# The
# Wonder-Under
## Book of
# christmas
# creations

LEISURE ARTS, INC., and OXMOOR HOUSE, INC.

# The Wonder-Under® Book of christmas creations

## EDITORIAL STAFF

**Vice President and Editor-in-Chief:** Anne Van Wagner Childs
**Executive Director:** Sandra Graham Case
**Editorial Director:** Susan Frantz Wiles
**Creative Art Director:** Gloria Bearden
**Senior Graphics Art Director:** Melinda Stout

### DESIGN
**Design Director:** Patricia Wallenfang Sowers
**Designers:** Sandra Spotts Ritchie, Anne Pulliam Stocks,
   Linda Diehl Tiano, Rebecca Sunwall Werle, and
   Katherine Prince Horton
**Executive Assistant:** Billie Steward

### EDITORIAL
**Managing Editor:** Linda L. Trimble
**Associate Editor:** Tammi Williamson Bradley
**Assistant Editors:** Terri Leming Davidson, Robyn Sheffield-Edwards,
   and Darla Burdette Kelsay
**Copy Editor:** Laura Lee Weland

### TECHNICAL
**Managing Editor:** Kristine Anderson Mertes
**Senior Technical Writer:** Barbara McClintock Vechik
**Associate Technical Writers:** Sherry Solida Ford, Diane Gillian Johns,
   and Christopher M. McCarty
**Production Assistant:** Sharon Heckel Gillam

### ART
**Book/Magazine Graphics Art Director:** Diane M. Hugo
**Graphics Illustrator:** M. Katherine Yancey
**Photography Stylists:** Pam Choate, Sondra Daniel, Aurora Huston,
   and Courtney Frazier Jones

### PROMOTIONS
**Managing Editors:** Tena Kelley Vaughn and Marjorie Ann Lacy
**Associate Editors:** Steven M. Cooper, Dixie L. Morris, and
   Jennifer Leigh Ertl
**Designer:** Dale T. Rowett
**Art Director:** Linda Lovette Smart
**Production Artist:** Leslie Loring Krebs
**Publishing Systems Administrator:** Cindy Lumpkin
**Publishing Systems Assistant:** Susan Mary Gray

## BUSINESS STAFF

**Publisher:** Bruce Akin
**Vice President, Marketing:** Guy A. Crossley
**Marketing Manager:** Byron L. Taylor
**Print Production Manager:** Laura Lockhart
**Vice President and General Manager:** Thomas L. Carlisle
**Retail Sales Director:** Richard Tignor

**Vice President, Retail Marketing:** Pam Stebbins
**Retail Marketing Director:** Margaret Sweetin
**Retail Customer Service Manager:** Carolyn Pruss
**General Merchandise Manager:** Russ Barnett
**Vice President, Finance:** Tom Siebenmorgen
**Distribution Director:** Ed M. Strackbein

Library of Congress Catalog Number 97-71086
Hardcover ISBN 0-8487-1607-8
Softcover ISBN 1-57486-062-3

# Introduction

**I**f you love crafting with fabric, The Wonder-Under® Book of Christmas Creations *is just for you! Leisure Arts and the makers of Pellon® Wonder-Under® Transfer Web, two leading names in the craft industry, are excited to present this collection of our very favorite holiday projects. It's the perfect combination — Leisure Arts' top-quality designs along with the ease of working with paper-backed fusible web and pre-cut tape! When you team Wonder-Under with basic fabric craft techniques, you can create tree-trimmers, decorative accents, and embellished clothing in no time. Adding appliqués becomes child's play — and you can even "hem" fabric without sewing a stitch! Just a press of the iron is all it takes to speed up your Christmas decorating and gift-giving. So choose your favorite festive prints, stripes, and plaids, and make this the most heartwarming holiday season ever!*

*Anne Childs*

# Table of Contents

## DRESSED IN HOLIDAY STYLE

# O CHRISTMAS TREE

# DECK THE HALLS

# GIFTS FOR ALL

# EVERY NOOK & CRANNY

# dressed in holiday style

**A**dd Christmas spirit to your family's wardrobe with this cheery collection of winter wearables! Designed to keep everyone dressed in holiday style, these fun projects are fast and easy to craft using Wonder-Under® transfer web. Just wait till you see how simple it is to turn plain sweatshirts, old vests, an ordinary muffler set, and more into festive holiday fashions. So, why not create these wonderful accessories and share the warmth of a handcrafted Christmas!

# HOLIDAY VESTS

*Oh, what fun it is to jazz up men's old suit vests to create cheery holiday fashions! Simply fuse Christmasy plaids onto a vest for him, and add a sprinkling of star appliqués and a prairie point edging to one for her.*

## Plaid Vest

**You will need:**
Wonder-Under® transfer web
men's suit vest
assorted plaid fabrics for vest front, binding, and pocket trim
replacement buttons (optional)
removable fabric marking pen
seam ripper
pressing cloth

**1.** Remove buttons from vest. Use seam ripper to take vest apart at shoulder and side seams.

**2.** Follow **Fusing Basics**, page 102, to press web to wrong side of desired fabrics for vest fronts. Place vest fronts, right side down, on paper side of fabrics. Draw around vest fronts; cut out. Fuse fabric pieces to vest fronts.

**3.** Follow **Binding**, page 102, to add 2¹/₂"w sewn binding to armholes and front edges.

**4.** For each pocket trim, cut a 2¹/₂" x 5¹/₄" strip of fabric. Press short, then long edges ¹/₄" to wrong side. Cut a piece of web slightly smaller than fabric strip; press to wrong side of fabric. Matching wrong sides, fold strip in half lengthwise; fuse together. Pin pocket trim to vest. Hand stitch in place along side and bottom edges.

**5.** To reassemble vest, insert shoulder and side seam allowances of vest fronts between lining and outer fabric of vest back. Topstitch through all layers.

**6.** On inside of vest, work narrow-width zigzag stitch with a very short stitch length around original buttonholes. Use seam ripper to open buttonholes.

**7.** Use removable pen to mark placement of buttons through buttonholes. Sew original or replacement buttons on vest.

## Prairie Points Vest

**You will need:**
Wonder-Under® transfer web
men's suit vest
assorted fabrics for appliqués and prairie points
one package ¹/₄"w double-fold bias tape to match vest
embroidery floss to match fabrics
tracing paper
pressing cloth

**1.** Using star pattern, follow **Making Appliqués**, page 102, to make seven star appliqués. If desired, cut several stars in reverse. Arrange stars on vest; fuse in place.

**2.** Using two strands of floss, work **Blanket Stitch**, page 104, around each appliqué.

**3.** To determine number of prairie points needed, measure edges of vest to be trimmed. The number of inches is equal to the number of prairie points needed. Cut a length of bias tape ¹/₂" longer than the determined measurement. Unfold short ends of bias tape and press ¹/₄" to wrong side. Refold bias tape.

**4.** For each prairie point, cut a 2" square from fabric. With wrong sides together, press square in half diagonally; press in half again (**Fig. 1**). Repeat to make number of prairie points determined in Step 3.

**Fig. 1**

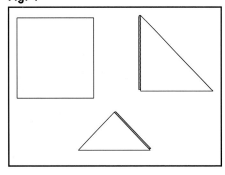

**5.** Overlap folded edge of two prairie points 1". Beginning at center of bias tape, insert raw edges of prairie points into fold of bias tape (**Fig. 2**); pin in place.

**Fig. 2**

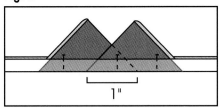

**6.** Insert folded edge of third prairie point 1" between open edges of one prairie point (**Fig. 3**). Repeat for remaining prairie points along each edge of bias tape. Stitching close to top edge, sew along length of bias tape.

**Fig. 3**

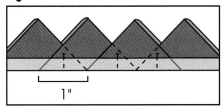

**7.** With prairie points extending ³/₄" beyond edges of vest, pin trim along inside edges of vest. Hand stitch in place.

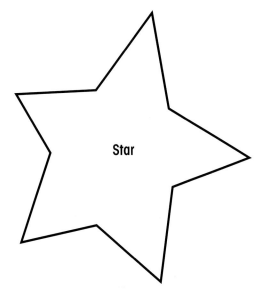

**Star**

# SWEETS CARDIGAN

*A ready-made cardigan takes on festive flair when it's embellished with candy cane and gingerbread man appliqués. Buttons, bows, and embroidery stitches trim these sweet motifs.*

**You will need:**
Wonder-Under® transfer web
cream knit cardigan
red and white striped and brown
    fabrics for appliqués
$1/4$"w grosgrain ribbon
$3/8$" dia. buttons
replacement buttons (optional)
red, brown, and cream embroidery
    floss
tracing paper
pressing cloth

**1.** Wash, dry, and press cardigan and fabrics.

**2.** Using patterns, page 107, follow **Making Appliqués**, page 102, to make four gingerbread man appliqués and five candy cane appliqués. If desired, cut several appliqués in reverse. Arrange appliqués on cardigan front; fuse in place.

**3.** Using three strands of red floss for candy canes and three strands of brown floss for gingerbread men, work **Blanket Stitch**, page 104, around each appliqué.

**4.** Using two strands of brown floss, work a **Cross Stitch**, page 105, for each eye and two strands of cream floss to work **Stem Stitch**, page 105, for "icing" on each gingerbread man.

**5.** For each gingerbread man, tie a 7" length of ribbon into a bow. Sew bow and two $3/8$" buttons to gingerbread man.

**6.** If desired, replace cardigan buttons.

# LITTLE ANGELS SWEATSHIRT

*A little girl will shine with Christmas spirit when she wears this angelic sweatshirt!*
*Featuring two heavenly helpers with Battenberg lace wings, this cute top is easy to create.*
*The fused-on fabric shapes are enhanced with dimensional paint and "gemstone" eyes.*

**You will need:**
- Wonder-Under® transfer web
- sweatshirt
- assorted fabrics for appliqués
- fusible interfacing (optional)
- two 4" lengths of 1/8"w satin ribbon
- Battenberg lace
- four 5mm acrylic stones for eyes
- gold micro glitter
- gold glitter dimensional paint
- dimensional paint to match fabrics
- T-shirt form
- powder blush for cheeks (optional)
- aluminum foil
- tracing paper
- rhinestone adhesive
- fabric glue
- pressing cloth

**1.** Wash, dry, and press sweatshirt and fabrics without using fabric softener.

**2.** Using patterns, page 107, follow **Making Appliqués**, page 102, to make two (one in reverse) each of hair, face, dress, shoe, and hand appliqués. For wands, follow **Foil Method**, page 102, to press web to one side of each ribbon length.

**3.** (**Note:** For Steps 3 and 5, refer to **Using Dimensional Paint**, page 106, for painting tips.) Trace star pattern, page 107, onto tracing paper. Use pattern to cut two stars from fabric. Use gold glitter paint and follow **Adding Glitter to Paint**, page 106, to paint stars.

**4.** For each set of wings, cut two pieces (two scallops each) of Battenberg lace. Arrange appliqués and wings on sweatshirt, overlapping as necessary; fuse in place. Use fabric glue to spot glue wings to secure and to glue stars at ends of wands; allow to dry.

**5.** Place shirt on shirt form. Use paints to outline and add details to appliqués; allow to dry.

**6.** Use rhinestone adhesive to glue stones to faces for eyes; allow to dry.

**7.** If desired, use fingertip to add dots of blush to faces for cheeks.

**8.** To launder shirt, turn shirt inside out and hand wash or machine wash on gentle cycle in cold water, using liquid fabric softener to keep paint soft. Turn shirt right side out and allow to air dry. Iron on wrong side only, avoiding design area.

# "BEARY" FUN SWEATSHIRT

*Transform a plain sweatshirt into fun winter wear for a little boy! Just fuse our daring ski bear onto the shirt and outfit him with a cozy scarf and ski poles.*

**You will need:**
Wonder-Under® transfer web
sweatshirt
assorted fabrics for appliqués
fusible interfacing (optional)
two 5³/₄" and two 1¹/₄" lengths of
   ¹/₈"w satin ribbon for ski poles
two 6" lengths of ³/₈"w grosgrain
   ribbon for skis
two 5mm acrylic stones for eyes
dimensional paint to match fabrics
T-shirt form
powder blush for cheeks (optional)
aluminum foil
tracing paper
rhinestone adhesive
fabric glue
pressing cloth

**1.** Wash, dry, and press sweatshirt and fabrics without using fabric softener.

**2.** Using patterns, page 108, follow **Making Appliqués**, page 102, to make two (one in reverse) each of hand and boot appliqués, and one each of pom-pom, hat, hat trim, head, ear, muzzle, scarf, sweater, sweater trim, and lower body appliqués.

**3.** Fold ends of grosgrain ribbon diagonally to right side for ski tips. Use fabric glue to glue tips in place; allow to dry. Follow **Foil Method**, page 102, to press web to wrong side of all ribbon lengths.

**4.** Arrange appliqués on sweatshirt, overlapping as necessary; fuse in place.

**5.** (**Note:** Refer to **Using Dimensional Paint**, page 106, for painting tips.) Place shirt on shirt form. Use paints to outline and add details to appliqués; allow to dry.

**6.** Use rhinestone adhesive to glue stones to face for eyes; allow to dry.

**7.** If desired, use fingertip to add dots of blush to face for cheeks.

**8.** Follow Step 8 of **Little Angels Sweatshirt**, page 10, to launder shirt.

# QUILTED CHRISTMAS JACKET

*This Christmas coat of many colors will certainly delight a quilt lover! The open-front jacket is fashioned by strip-piecing a variety of red and green fabrics over a men's shirt. For a quilted look, a layer of batting is fused to the shirt before the strips are added.*

**You will need:**
Wonder-Under® transfer web
men's long-sleeve button-front shirt
1 yd **each** of six coordinating 44/45"w cotton fabrics for strips
fabric for bias binding
low-loft polyester bonded batting
removable fabric marking pen
seam ripper
yardstick
pressing cloth

## PREPARING THE SHIRT

**Note:** Use seam ripper for removal of all shirt pieces and opening of seams.

**1.** Wash, dry, and press shirt and fabrics.

**2.** To determine sleeve lengths, put on shirt. With arms at sides, mark desired sleeve lengths.

**3.** Remove pockets, pocket flaps, cuffs, and labels from shirt.

**4.** Marking button placement on wrong side of center front as each button is removed, remove buttons. Use yardstick to draw a line through marks down shirt front.

**5.** Remove collar and collar band.

**6.** Remove sleeves from shirt and open seams of sleeves. Label right and left sleeves on wrong sides. Press sleeves flat. Zigzag stitch sleeve placket openings closed (**Fig. 1**).

**Fig. 1**

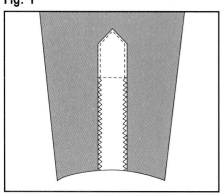

**7.** Use yardstick to draw a line straight across each sleeve at point marked in Step 2; cut along drawn lines.

**8.** Match bottom edges of shirt fronts and back. Use yardstick to draw a line straight across bottom of shirt directly above hem. Cutting through both layers, cut along drawn line.

**9.** With bottom edges of shirt fronts and back even, press a crease at each shoulder. Cut along each crease.

**10.** Open side seams of shirt. Label right and left shirt fronts and shirt back on wrong sides.

**11.** Remove buttonhole placket from shirt front; press shirt front flat.

**12.** Remove stitching from facing on remaining shirt front; press shirt front flat.

**13.** Matching right sides, place shirt fronts together. Cut through both layers along line drawn in Step 4.

**14.** Press shirt back flat. If shirt has pleats in back, zigzag stitch over folds created by pleats to bottom edge (**Fig. 2**).

**Fig. 2**

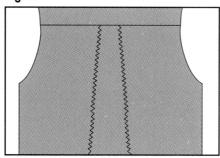

## CONSTRUCTING THE JACKET

**Note:** For all machine stitching, match right sides and raw edges and use a 1/4" seam allowance.

**1.** Trim selvages from each fabric. Cut strips of fabric in varying widths from 1 1/2"w to 2 1/2"w.

**2.** Using shirt sections as patterns, cut one piece of batting and one piece of web for each shirt section. Follow **Fusing Basics**, page 102, to press web to right side of each corresponding shirt piece. Fuse batting to each shirt piece.

**3.** Use yardstick to draw a vertical line on batting down center of shirt back.

**4.** Place one fabric strip right side up on batting with one long edge of strip along drawn line.

**5.** Place one long edge of a second fabric strip along one long edge of first strip; pin in place (**Fig. 3**). Stitch strip in place through all layers. Flip second strip right side up; press.

**Fig. 3**

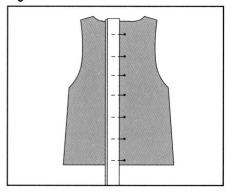

**6.** Using additional fabric strips, repeat Step 5 until half of shirt back is covered.

**7.** Turn shirt back upside down. Follow Steps 5 and 6 to cover remaining half of shirt back.

**8.** Repeat Steps 3 - 7 for sleeve and front pieces.

**9.** To hold ends of fabric strips in place, baste 1/8" from edges of each shirt section.

**10.** Trim ends of strips even with edges of shirt pieces.

**11.** Stitch shirt fronts to shirt back at shoulders.

**12.** Stitch each sleeve to jacket, easing sleeve to fit; press seams open.

**13.** Stitch each side and underarm seam; press seams open.

**14.** Trim lower edge of jacket to straighten, if necessary.

**15.** Follow **Binding**, page 102, to add $2^1/_2$"w sewn binding to neck, front, and bottom edges and to each sleeve.

13

# GINGERBREAD WARMERS

*Warm up a ready-made muffler set with friendly gingerbread men and heart appliqués. Attached with fusible web, the adorable motifs are trimmed with blanket stitching for a homey finishing touch.*

**1.** Using patterns, page 109, follow **Making Appliqués**, page 102, to make one each of gingerbread man and large heart appliqués for scarf, three gingerbread man appliqués for cap, and two small heart appliqués for mittens.

**2.** Arrange appliqués on scarf, cap, and mittens; fuse in place.

**3.** Using three strands of brown floss for gingerbread men and three strands of red floss for hearts, work **Blanket Stitch**, page 104, around each appliqué. Using six strands of brown floss, work a **French Knot**, page 105, for each eye on each gingerbread man.

**4.** For each gingerbread man, tie a 7" length of ribbon into a bow. Sew bow to gingerbread man.

# SWEET BABY JACKET

*Your little one will look so sweet in this playful Christmas cardigan! Crafted from an infant-size sweatshirt, the cute cover-up is trimmed with fused-on rickrack and fabric appliqués.*

## You will need:
- Wonder-Under® transfer web
- infant sweatshirt
- assorted fabrics for appliqués
- one package jumbo rickrack
- tear-away stabilizer
- aluminum foil
- red and black permanent fabric pens
- removable fabric marking pen
- pinking shears
- clear nylon thread
- ruler
- pressing cloth

**1.** Wash, dry, and press sweatshirt and fabrics.

**2.** For front opening, use ruler and removable pen to draw a line down center front of shirt. Use pinking shears to cut shirt open along line.

**3.** If needed, use pinking shears to cut ribbed waistband from shirt.

**4.** Measure each front, neckline, and bottom edge. Cut pieces of rickrack the determined measurements. Follow **Foil Method**, page 102, press web to one side of each rickrack piece. Fuse rickrack along edges of shirt.

**5.** Using clear thread and zigzag stitch, sew over rickrack to secure.

### Diagram

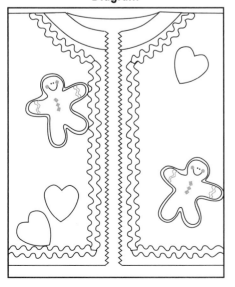

**6.** Using patterns, page 109, follow **Making Appliqués**, page 102, to make two each of gingerbread boy and gingerbread boy background appliqués and three small heart appliqués.

**7.** Refer to **Diagram** to arrange appliqués on sweatshirt, overlapping as necessary; fuse in place.

**8.** Using clear thread, follow **Machine Appliqué**, page 105, to stitch over raw edges of appliqués.

**9.** Using permanent pens, add details to gingerbread boys.

# STARRY FOREST CARDIGAN

*This festive cardigan, made from a sweatshirt, features a forest of appliquéd evergreens decorated with blanket stitching. Stars created with straight stitches are scattered above the trees, and coordinating fabric trims the edges of the jacket.*

**You will need:**
Wonder-Under® transfer web
sweatshirt
assorted fabrics for trees and
    binding
three ⅝" dia. buttons for cuffs and
    neckline
assorted buttons for treetops
embroidery floss to match fabrics
    and for stars
fabric marking pen
yardstick
pressing cloth

**1.** Wash, dry, and press sweatshirt and fabrics.

**2.** For front opening, use pen and yardstick to draw a line down center front of shirt. Cut shirt open along drawn line.

**3.** Remove neck and waist ribbings; cut sleeves to desired length.

**4.** Follow **Binding**, page 102, to add 2½"w sewn binding to neck, front, and bottom edges and to each sleeve and to make a 1"w x 3½"l strip of binding for button loop.

**5.** Unfold button loop strip, press ends ½" to wrong side; refold strip. Topstitch along each long edge. Form a loop and sew ends to wrong side of cardigan at top of right front. Sew button to left edge.

**6.** For cuff on each sleeve, make a 1" pleat in sleeve (**Fig. 1**) and sew button to sleeve over pleat.

Fig. 1

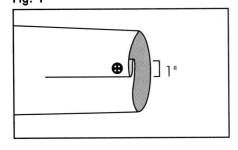

**7.** Using patterns, page 109, follow **Making Appliqués**, page 102, to make four each of tree A and tree B appliqués, and five tree C appliqués.

**8.** Refer to **Diagram**, page 110, to arrange appliqués along lower edge of cardigan; fuse in place.

**9.** Using three strands of floss, work **Blanket Stitch**, page 104, around each appliqué. Using two strands of floss, work **Straight Stitch**, page 105, for stars.

**10.** Sew a button to top of each tree.

# FESTIVE TIES

*It's quick and easy to add Yuletide pizzazz to men's neckties! Just fuse on
a Santa or snowman cutout and embellish with simple blanket stitching.*

## Santa Tie

**You will need:**
Heavy Duty Wonder-Under®
    transfer web
tie (we used a flannel tie)
assorted felt for appliqués
embroidery floss to match felt
thread to match tie
seam ripper
pressing cloth

**1.** Using patterns, page 110, follow
**Making Appliqués**, page 102, to
make one each of coat, face, beard,
mitten A, mitten B, boots, tree, and
tree trunk appliqués. Arrange
appliqués on tie, overlapping as
necessary; fuse in place.

**2.** Use seam ripper to open back
seam of tie behind Santa.

**3.** Using three strands of floss, work
**Blanket Stitch**, page 104, around
coat, beard, boots, and tree appliqués.

**4.** Restitch back seam of tie.

## Snowman Tie

**You will need:**
Heavy Duty Wonder-Under®
    transfer web
tie (we used a flannel tie)
felt for hat and snowman appliqués
flannel fabric for scarf appliqué
black embroidery floss
thread to match tie
seam ripper
pressing cloth

**1.** Using patterns, page 110, follow
**Making Appliqués**, page 102, to
make one each of snowman and hat
appliqués from felt, and one scarf
appliqué from flannel fabric. Arrange
appliqués on tie, overlapping as
necessary; fuse in place.

**2.** Use seam ripper to open back
seam of tie behind snowman.

**3.** Using three strands of floss, work a
**Cross Stitch**, page 105, for each eye;
**Running Stitch**, page 105, for mouth;
and **Blanket Stitch**, page 104, around
each appliqué, stopping ¹/₈" from
ends of scarf. Fray ends of scarf.

**4.** Restitch back seam of tie.

# CHEERY APRONS

*Cooking up holiday fun is easy with these Christmas aprons! For Mom, there's a ruffled apron sewn with cheery fabrics and embellished with machine appliqué. For her little kitchen helper, a purchased chef's apron is accented with a fused-on message and colorful trim.*

## Holiday House Apron

**You will need:**
Wonder-Under® transfer web
two $9^1/_2$" squares of fabric for bib
$22^1/_2$" x $39^1/_2$" fabric piece for skirt
1 yd of 44/45"w fabric for ties and ruffles
assorted fabrics for appliqués
$9^1/_2$" square of lightweight fusible interfacing
three $^3/_8$" dia. round shank buttons for berries
removable fabric marking pen
clear nylon thread
thread to match fabrics
pressing cloth

**1.** Follow manufacturer's instructions to fuse interfacing to wrong side of one $9^1/_2$" fabric square.

**2.** Using patterns, page 110, follow **Making Appliqués**, page 102, to make one each of heart, roof, house side, house front, and door appliqués; two chimney appliqués; and twelve (five in reverse) leaf appliqués. Center and arrange appliqués on right side of interfaced fabric square, overlapping as necessary; fuse in place.

**3.** Using clear thread, follow **Machine Appliqué**, page 105, to stitch over raw edges of appliqués.

**4.** Sew buttons between leaves.

**5.** (**Note:** Use a $^1/_2$" seam allowance for all sewing steps, unless otherwise indicated.) For bib ruffle, cut a 4" x 68" strip of fabric (pieced as necessary).

**6.** Matching wrong sides, press strip in half lengthwise. Baste $^1/_4$" and $^1/_2$" from long raw edge. Pull basting threads to gather.

**7.** Matching right sides and raw edges, pin ruffle to top and sides of appliquéd square; adjust gathers to fit and baste in place.

**8.** To complete bib, match right sides and raw edges of fabric squares. Leaving bottom edge open for turning, sew squares together. Clip corners and trim seams. Turn right side out and remove basting threads; press.

**9.** Using a 4" x 94" strip of fabric (pieced as necessary), refer to Step 6 to make skirt ruffle.

**10.** Matching right sides and raw edges, pin ruffle to bottom of skirt; adjust gathers to fit and sew in place. Press seam toward skirt.

**11.** Press each side of skirt and ruffle $^1/_2$" to wrong side. Press $^1/_2$" to wrong side again; sew in place.

**12.** Measure $5^1/_2$" from each side on top edge of skirt; mark with removable pen (**Fig. 1**). Baste $^1/_4$" and $^1/_2$" from raw edge of skirt between marks.

**Fig. 1**

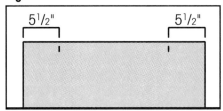

**13.** Mark center on bottom of bib and top of skirt. Matching right sides, raw edges, and centers, pin bib to top edge of skirt between marks. Pull basting threads to gather. Adjust gathers to fit bib; sew bib to skirt.

**14.** Cut a $2^1/_2$" x 72" strip of fabric (pieced as necessary) for ties at waist and two 2" x 28" strips for ties at neck. For each strip, press short edges of each strip $^1/_2$" to wrong side. Matching wrong sides, press strip in half lengthwise; unfold. Press long edges to center; refold strip.

**15.** For ties at waist, measure $23^1/_2$" from one end of strip; mark with removable pen. Beginning at mark, insert raw edge of skirt and bib into fold of strip; pin. Sew close to pressed edges of strip from end to end. Press seam toward bib.

**16.** For ties at neck, sew close to pressed edges of each strip; sew one end of each tie to wrong side of bib.

## Ho-Ho-Ho Apron

**You will need:**
Heavy Duty Wonder-Under® transfer web
child's chef's apron
fabric for trim
assorted fabrics for appliqués
tear-away stabilizer
three 10" ribbon lengths for bows
three 13mm jingle bells
three safety pins
thread to match trim fabric
clear nylon thread
pressing cloth

**1.** Wash, dry, and press fabrics and apron.

**2.** Using patterns, page 110, follow **Making Appliqués**, page 102, to make three each of "H" and "O" appliqués. Arrange appliqués on apron as desired; fuse in place.

**3.** Using clear thread, follow **Machine Appliqué**, page 105, to stitch over raw edges of appliqués.

**4.** For trim, measure outside edge of apron; add $1^1/_2$". Cut a 1"w bias strip the determined measurement (pieced as necessary). Press one end of strip $^1/_2$" to wrong side. Matching wrong sides, press strip in half lengthwise; unfold. Matching wrong sides, press long edges to center.

**5.** Beginning with unpressed end, pin trim to apron, mitering corners as necessary. Topstitch close to each edge of trim.

**6.** Tie each ribbon length into a bow. Sew one bell to center of each bow. Use safety pin to pin one bow to top center of each "O."

**7.** Remove bows to launder.

# JOLLY SWEATSHIRTS

*Brighten the season for two special youngsters with these jolly appliqué projects! Decorated with pom-poms and beads, Santa and his smiling snow buddy are a breeze to fuse in place.*

## Snowman Sweatshirt

**You will need:**
Wonder-Under® transfer web
child's sweatshirt
assorted fabrics for appliqués
fusible interfacing (optional)
tear-away stabilizer
$7/8$" pom-pom for hat
two 4mm beads for eyes
thread to match fabrics
pressing cloth

**1.** Wash, dry, and press sweatshirt and fabrics.

**2.** Using patterns, page 111, follow **Making Appliqués**, page 102, to make one each of snowman hat, snowman hat trim/body, scarf, and broom appliqués. Arrange appliqués on sweatshirt, overlapping as necessary; fuse in place.

**3.** Using coordinating color thread for each appliqué, follow **Machine Appliqué**, page 105, to stitch over raw edges of appliqués. Using grey lines on patterns as a guide, use a medium-width zigzag stitch with a very short stitch length to add buttons, broom handle, and details around hat trim, body, hand, and scarf. Using machine straight stitch, add mouth to face and detail lines on broom.

**4.** Sew beads to face for eyes.

**5.** Sew pom-pom to tip of hat.

## Santa Sweatshirt

**You will need:**
Wonder-Under® transfer web
child's sweatshirt
assorted fabrics for appliqués
fusible interfacing (optional)
tear-away stabilizer
two 4mm beads for eyes
$7/8$" pom-pom for hat
$1/2$" pom-pom for nose
thread to match fabrics
pressing cloth

**1.** Wash, dry, and press sweatshirt and fabrics.

**2.** Using patterns, page 111, follow **Making Appliqués**, page 102, to make one each of Santa hat trim/beard, face, and Santa hat appliqués. Arrange appliqués on sweatshirt, overlapping as necessary; fuse in place.

**3.** Using coordinating color thread for each appliqué, follow **Machine Appliqué**, page 105, to stitch over raw edges of appliqués. Using grey lines as a guide, use a medium-width zigzag stitch with a very short stitch length to add mouth and detail lines to hat and mustache.

**4.** Sew beads to face for eyes.

**5.** Sew $7/8$" pom-pom to tip of hat and $1/2$" pom-pom to face for nose.

# HOLLY HEART SWEATSHIRT

*Adorned with a heart-shaped holly wreath in shades of red, green, and gold, this sweatshirt will make
your holiday celebration extra special! And with our no-sew appliqué technique, it's a pleasure to create.*

**You will need:**
Wonder-Under® transfer web
sweatshirt
green dotted, red/green striped,
    green check, and red dotted
    fabrics for appliqués
gold micro glitter
gold glitter dimensional paint
T-shirt form
tracing paper
pressing cloth

**1.** Wash, dry, and press shirt and fabrics without using fabric softener.

**2.** Using patterns, page 112, follow **Making Appliqués**, page 102, to make seven each of A and B appliqués and eight C appliqués from green dotted fabric; two (one in reverse) each of E and F appliqués from red/green striped fabric; six B appliqués from green check fabric; and ten D appliqués from red dotted fabric.

**3.** Refer to **Diagram** to arrange appliqués on shirt, overlapping as necessary; fuse in place.

### Diagram

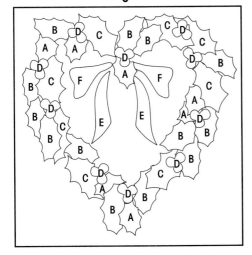

**4.** (**Note:** Refer to **Using Dimensional Paint**, page 106, for painting tips.) Place shirt on shirt form and follow **Adding Glitter To Paint**, page 106, to paint outlines and to add details to appliqués.

**5.** To launder shirt, turn shirt inside out and hand wash or machine wash on gentle cycle in cold water, using liquid fabric softener to keep paint soft. Turn shirt right side out and allow to air dry. Iron on wrong side only, avoiding design area.

# CHRISTMAS SAMPLER SWEATSHIRT

*A sampling of favorite holiday motifs adorns this Christmas sweatshirt. To create the clever top, replace the front of an ordinary sweatshirt with our pieced fabric design. It'll spread country cheer wherever it's worn!*

## You will need:

Wonder-Under® transfer web
sweatshirt with set-in sleeves and no side seams (we used a women's-size medium shirt)
fabrics for piecing shirt front (see **Table**)
fabrics for appliqués
27" x 32" piece of muslin for shirt front backing
fusible interfacing
tear-away stabilizer
³/₈" dia. red shank button
removable fabric marking pen
seam ripper
clear nylon thread
black thread
thread to match shirt
tracing paper
yardstick
pressing cloth

**Note:** For all sewing, match right sides and raw edges and use a ¹/₄" seam allowance, unless otherwise indicated.

## PIECING SHIRT FRONT

**1.** Wash, dry, and press shirt and fabrics.

**2.** Refer to **Table** to cut fabrics for piecing shirt front.

**3.** Matching long edges, fold muslin in half; press.

**4.** (**Note:** For Steps 4 - 9, refer to **Assembly Diagram**.) Sew A, B, C, and D together. With top edge of A 5" below one short edge (top edge) of muslin, center A-B-C-D, right side up, over crease in muslin; pin in place.

**5.** Sew E, F, and G together.

**6.** Place E-F-G, right side down, on A-D, matching left edge of E to right edge of A-D.

**7.** Sewing through all layers along matched edges, sew pieces together. Flip E-G right side up; press.

**8.** Sew H and I together. Repeat Step 7 to sew top edge of H-I to bottom edge of D-G.

**9.** Sew J, K, and L together. Repeat Step 7 to sew right edge of J-K-L to left edges of A-D and H-I.

**10.** Repeat Step 7 to sew M, N, O, then P to previously sewn pieces, completing pieced front. Baste outer edges of M, N, O, and P to muslin.

## APPLIQUÉING SHIRT FRONT

**1.** Matching grey lines and arrows, trace tree top and tree bottom patterns, page 112, onto tracing paper. Using patterns, pages 112 and 113, and full-size tree pattern, follow **Making Appliqués**, page 102, to make two star A appliqués and one each of tree, tree trunk, star B, star C, face, beard, hat trim, hat, pom-pom, bow, "N," "O," "E," and "L" appliqués.

**2.** Arrange appliqués on shirt front, overlapping as necessary; fuse in place.

**3.** Using clear thread, follow **Machine Appliqué**, page 105, to stitch over raw edges of appliqués.

**4.** For Santa's mustache, tear two 1" x 3" pieces from fabric; layer fabric pieces together. Gather pieces at center. Place mustache on Santa and use a medium-width zigzag stitch with a very short stitch length to stitch over gathered center. Sew button to face for nose.

**5.** Referring to patterns, use removable pen to mark placement of eyes on Santa and draw details on bow. Use black thread and a medium-width zigzag stitch with a very short stitch length to stitch eyes. Use a narrow-width zigzag stitch with a very short stitch length to stitch details on bow.

## ATTACHING SHIRT FRONT TO SHIRT

**1.** To mark cutting lines for removing front of shirt, use removable pen and yardstick to draw a line down front of shirt from underarm seam to waist ribbing ¹/₄" from each side fold (**Fig. 1**).

**Fig. 1**

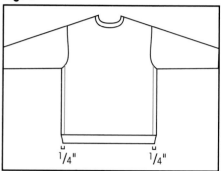

**2.** Use removable pen to mark center front and back and positions of shoulder seams on neck ribbing. Mark center front and back on waist ribbing.

**3.** Use seam ripper to remove neck and waist ribbings, take shoulder seams apart, and take each armhole seam apart at front of shirt from shoulder seam to drawn line at side of shirt. Cut away shirt front along drawn lines.

**4.** Using original shirt as pattern, center and pin shirt front, right side up, on pieced shirt front; cut out pieced shirt front.

**5.** (**Note:** Sew along previous seamlines unless otherwise indicated, easing pieces to fit as necessary.) Sew pieced shirt front to shirt back at shoulders and sides. Sew sleeves to shirt front. Turn shirt right side out; press.

**6.** Use removable pen to mark center front and back on neck edge and bottom edge of shirt. Matching marks on ribbings to shoulder seams and marks on shirt, pin ribbings to shirt; sew in place.

## TABLE

| Piece | Size (width x length) |
|-------|----------------------|
| A | 5$\frac{1}{2}$" x 3$\frac{3}{4}$" |
| B | 5$\frac{1}{2}$" x 10$\frac{1}{2}$" |
| C | 5$\frac{1}{2}$" x 1$\frac{1}{4}$" |
| D | 5$\frac{1}{2}$" x 1" |
| E | 3$\frac{1}{2}$" x 15" |
| F | 1$\frac{1}{2}$" x 15" |
| G | 2$\frac{1}{2}$" x 15" |
| H | 11$\frac{1}{2}$" x 6$\frac{1}{4}$" |
| I | 11$\frac{1}{2}$" x 1$\frac{3}{4}$" |
| J | 6$\frac{1}{2}$" x 6$\frac{1}{4}$" |
| K | 6$\frac{1}{2}$" x 1$\frac{1}{2}$" |
| L | 6$\frac{1}{2}$" x 15$\frac{1}{4}$" |
| M | 4" x 22" |
| N | 21" x 4$\frac{1}{2}$" |
| O | 4$\frac{1}{2}$" x 26" |
| P | 25" x 4$\frac{1}{2}$" |

## Assembly Diagram

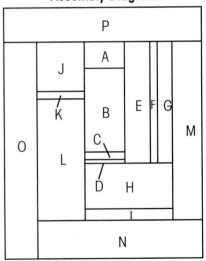

# COZY MITTENS CARDIGAN

*Welcome winter weather wearing this whimsical cardigan made from an adult-size sweatshirt. With its ribbings removed from the neck, waist, and sleeves, the jacket is embellished with fused-on mitten appliqués, buttons, and simple embroidery stitches.*

**You will need:**
Wonder-Under® transfer web
sweatshirt with set-in sleeves
assorted fabrics for appliqués
one package 1/2" wide double-fold
    bias tape for facing
embroidery floss to match fabrics
buttons for cuffs and decoration
fabric marking pen
thread to match shirt
yardstick
pressing cloth

**1.** Follow Steps 1 - 3 of **Starry Forest Cardigan**, page 16, to prepare and cut sweatshirt.

**2.** For facings, measure front, neckline, and bottom edges (**Fig. 1**); add 1" to measurement. Cut a piece of bias tape the determined measurement. Repeat for each sleeve.

**Fig. 1**

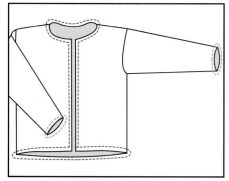

**3.** Unfold one edge of one facing, press one end 1/2" to wrong side. Matching right sides and raw edges and beginning with unpressed end at center back, pin facing to bottom, front, and neckline edges. Using a 1/2" seam allowance, stitch facing to shirt. Press facing to wrong side of shirt; topstitch to secure facing. Repeat for each sleeve.

**4.** Follow Step 6 of **Starry Forest Cardigan**, page 16, to make cuffs.

**5.** Using patterns, page 113, follow **Making Appliqués**, page 102, to make desired number of mitten, mitten tip, cuff, heart, and pointed star appliqués. Arrange appliqués on cardigan, overlapping as necessary; fuse in place.

**6.** Using three strands of floss, work **Running Stitch**, page 105, for strings connecting mittens and **Blanket Stitch**, page 104, around each edge of cardigan and each appliqué.

**7.** Arrange buttons on cardigan as desired; sew in place.

# JOY APRON

*A little fabric and fusible web transform a purchased chef's apron into a darling Christmas accessory. Because appliquéing the simple shapes is so quick and easy, you'll want to make several for gifts (and keep one for yourself). The reindeer adds a touch of whimsy to the cheery holiday message: Joy — to the world!*

**You will need:**
Heavy Duty Wonder-Under® transfer web
chef's apron
assorted fabrics for appliqués
tear-away stabilizer
3¹/₂" of ³/₈"w red grosgrain ribbon
3¹/₂" of ⁵/₈"w green grosgrain ribbon
³/₄" dia. red shank button for nose
two ¹/₄" dia. black shank buttons for eyes
aluminum foil
clear nylon thread
pressing cloth

**1.** Wash, dry, and press fabrics and apron.

**2.** Using patterns, page 114, follow **Making Appliqués**, page 102, to make one each of "J," "Y," reindeer face, antler A, and antler B appliqués.

**3.** Follow **Foil Method**, page 102, to press web to one side of each ribbon length.

**4.** Remove paper backing from red ribbon; center and fuse red ribbon to green ribbon. Referring to pattern for placement, trim ends of ribbons even with sides of reindeer face. Remove paper backing from green ribbon; fuse green ribbon to face.

**5.** Referring to **Diagram**, page 114, arrange appliqués on apron, overlapping as necessary; fuse in place.

**6.** Using clear thread, follow **Machine Appliqué**, page 105, to stitch over raw edges of appliqués.

**7.** Sew buttons to reindeer face for eyes and nose.

# o christmas tree

**A** *gaily decked tree is the highlight of the holiday home. Cherished mementos of Christmases past are lovingly nestled among rich evergreen boughs along with new trinkets to delight and fill us with holiday spirit. In this wondrous selection, you'll discover all you need to dress your tree, from fanciful toppers and quick-to-make ornaments to country angels and charming skirts. Let us help you make this Christmas tree the merriest ever!*

# SNOWMAN TREE

*A jaunty top hat crafted from an oatmeal box makes a cute topper for our snowman tree.*
*This fun ensemble includes flying snowman and mitten ornaments cut from fabric-covered*
*poster board. A bead garland studded with fabric-covered star shapes is draped around*
*the tree, and icicles fashioned from round wooden clothespins glisten with new-fallen "snow."*

## Star Garland

**You will need:**
Wonder-Under® transfer web
wooden bead garland
assorted fabrics for star appliqués
yellow acrylic paint
paintbrush
decorative buttons
black permanent pen
poster board
hot glue gun and glue sticks
pressing cloth

**1.** Using star pattern, page 115, follow **Making Appliqués**, page 102, to make desired number of star appliqués.

**2.** Fuse star appliqués to poster board; cut out.

**3.** Use paint to paint poster board side of each star; allow to dry.

**4.** Use pen to draw "stitches" along edges on painted side of each star.

**5.** Glue one button to fabric side of each star.

**6.** Glue painted side of each star to garland.

## Icicle Ornaments

**Note:** Supplies are for making one ornament.

**You will need:**
3³/₄" long round wooden clothespin
snow texturing medium
paintbrush
mica flakes
¹/₂"w masking tape
aluminum foil
clear nylon thread
hot glue gun and glue sticks

**1.** Shape a small piece of foil around bottom of clothespin to form an icicle shape (**Fig. 1**).

**Fig. 1**

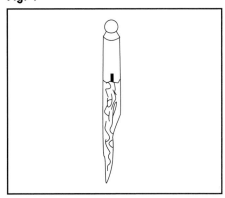

**2.** Beginning just above slit in clothespin and ending at tip of foil shape, wrap icicle shape with masking tape.

**3.** Use paintbrush to apply snow texturing medium to icicle; roll in mica flakes. Allow to dry.

**4.** For hanger, cut an 8" length of clear thread. Fold in half and knot ends together. Glue knot to icicle.

## Top Hat Tree Topper

**You will need:**
Heavy Duty Wonder-Under® transfer web
42-oz. cylinder-shaped oatmeal box 9¹/₂"h x 5" dia.
¹/₃ yd of 72"w black felt
fabric for hatband
2¹/₄"w wooden star
button
yellow acrylic paint
paintbrush
poster board
black permanent pen
removable fabric marking pen
compass
craft knife
hot glue gun and glue sticks
pressing cloth

**1.** For top of hat, draw a line around box 5" from bottom; use craft knife to cut along drawn line.

**2.** Measure around box; add ¹/₂". Cut one 5"w piece of felt and one 1³/₄"w strip of web by the determined measurement.

**3.** For hatband, follow **Fusing Basics**, page 102, to press web strip to wrong side of fabric. Cut out fabric along edges of web. Matching long edges, fuse hatband along one edge of felt piece.

**4.** With hatband even with open end of box, glue felt piece around box.

**5.** Using top of hat as a pattern, draw a circle on felt using removable pen; cut out. Glue felt circle to top of hat.

**6.** For hat brim, cut two 11" squares each from felt and web. Press web to one side of each felt square.

**7.** Use compass to draw a 10¹/₄" dia. circle on poster board. Center bottom of hat top on circle and draw inner circle; cut along drawn lines.

**8.** Trace around poster board ring on paper side of each felt square.

**9.** For top of brim, cut ring from one felt square.

**10.** For bottom of brim, cut along outer circle of remaining felt square. Cut ³/₄" inside inner circle. Make clips to ¹/₈" from drawn inner circle (**Fig. 1**).

**Fig. 1**

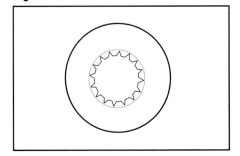

**11.** Trim ¹/₄" from outer edge of poster board ring.

**12.** Place poster board ring between top and bottom felt rings; fuse in place.

**13.** Center top of hat on top of brim; glue in place.

**14.** Glue clipped edges to inside of hat.

**15.** Paint star yellow; allow to dry. Use pen to draw "stitches" along edges of star. Glue button to star. Glue star to hatband.

# Mitten Ornaments

**Note:** Supplies are for making one ornament.

**You will need:**
Heavy Duty Wonder-Under® transfer web
felt for mitten appliqués
fabric for heart appliqués
sock cuff or knit ribbing for trim
poster board
16" length of jute twine
tracing paper
hot glue gun and glue sticks
pressing cloth

**1.** Using patterns, page 115, follow **Making Appliqués**, page 102, to make four (two in reverse) mitten appliqués from felt, and two heart appliqués from fabric.

**2.** Trace mitten insert pattern, page 115, onto tracing paper. Use pattern to cut two mitten inserts from poster board.

**3.** For each mitten, place one mitten insert between one pair of felt mittens; fuse together.

**4.** Fuse one heart appliqué to front of each mitten.

**5.** For trim on each mitten, cut one 1³/₄" x 2¹/₂" strip from sock cuff. Fold in half lengthwise and place fold over cuff of mitten; glue in place. Trim ends (**Fig. 1**).

**Fig. 1**

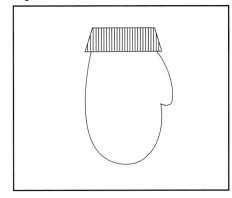

**6.** For hanger, fold jute in half and knot 6" from ends to form a 2" loop. Tack one end of jute to back of each mitten.

# Flying Snowman Ornaments

**Note:** Supplies are for making one ornament.

**You will need:**
Heavy Duty Wonder-Under® transfer web
cotton batting for snowman and arm appliqués
fabrics for vest, boot, and scarf appliqués
felt for hat appliqué
2¹/₄"w wooden star
9" long twig
yellow acrylic paint
paintbrush
buttons for eye, cheek, and vest
jute twine
black permanent pen
orange colored pencil
poster board
tracing paper
hot glue gun and glue sticks
pressing cloth

**1.** Using patterns, page 115, follow **Making Appliqués**, page 102, to make one each of arm and entire snowman appliqués from batting; one each of vest, boot, and scarf appliqués from fabrics; and one hat appliqué from felt. If desired, make appliqués in reverse for a snowman facing opposite direction.

**2.** Fuse snowman and arm appliqués to poster board; cut out. Fuse vest, boot, and hat appliqués to snowman.

**3.** Trace arm and nose patterns, page 115, onto tracing paper. Use patterns to cut one arm and one nose from poster board.

**4.** For fringe, cut three 1" pieces of jute. Separate into strands and glue to front of scarf edge on poster board (**Fig. 1**). Fuse scarf appliqué to snowman.

**Fig. 1**

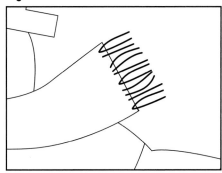

**5.** Glue batting arm to front of snowman, poster board arm to back of snowman, and buttons to vest and to face for eye and cheek.

**6.** Use pencil to color poster board nose orange; glue to face.

**7.** For wand, paint star yellow; allow to dry. Use pen to draw "stitches" along edges of star. Glue star to twig. Glue twig between arms.

# COUNTRY ANGELS

*Share the seasonal message of love, peace, and joy with these delightful country angels.*
*Crafted over foam balls, the roly-poly pretties feature wings and stars created by fusing*
*fabric appliqués to poster board. Curly doll hair and pen "stitching" add to their appeal.*

**Note:** Supplies are for making one ornament.

**You will need:**
Wonder-Under® transfer web
12" square of fabric
assorted fabrics for wings, star, and face appliqués
3" dia. foam ball
braided doll hair
14" length of gold wired cord
poster board
cosmetic blush
black, red, and brown permanent pens
string
pinking shears
compass
rubber band
hot glue gun and glue sticks
pressing cloth

**1.** Use compass to draw an 11¹/₂" dia. circle on fabric square. Use pinking shears to cut out circle.

**2.** Gather fabric circle tightly around foam ball; secure gathers with rubber band. Tie string into a bow over rubber band.

**3.** Using patterns, page 116, follow **Making Appliqués**, page 102, to make two wings appliqués and one each of medium star, small star, and angel head appliqués.

**4.** Fuse one wings, medium star, and angel head appliqués to poster board; cut out. Fuse small star appliqué to center of medium star and remaining wings appliqué to poster board side of wings.

**5.** Use pens to draw face on head; write "Love," "Peace," or "Joy" at center of small star; and draw "stitches" along edges of small star and wings.

**6.** Glue star to front of fabric-covered ball.

**7.** Use fingertip to apply blush to cheeks. Cut a 4" length of doll hair; unbraid hair. Center and glue hair to top of head; fluff ends of hair.

**8.** Insert angel head in center of gathers on fabric-covered ball; glue in place.

**9.** Glue wings to gathers on back of fabric-covered ball.

**10.** For halo, beginning 1" from one end of cord, form two 1" dia. circles. Wrap "tail" of cord around back of circles to hold circles together. Twist ends together. With halo positioned over angel's head, glue ends to back of head.

# CRAZY-QUILT TREE SKIRT

*Our Victorian tree skirt allows you to enjoy the look of quilting without sewing a stitch! Christmas fabrics are simply fused to a piece of muslin and accented with dimensional paint "stitching."*

**You will need:**
Wonder-Under® transfer web
44" square of muslin
assorted fabric scraps for crazy quilt pieces
fabric for binding
3³/₄ yds of 1" long gold fringe
3³/₄ yds of ¹/₄"w velvet ribbon
gold dimensional paint
removable fabric marking pen
string
thumbtack
pencil
fabric glue
pressing cloth

**1.** Follow **Fusing Basics**, page 102, to press web to wrong sides of fabric scraps. Overlapping edges ¹/₄" and trimming to fit, arrange fabric scraps on muslin. Fuse in place.

**2.** Matching right sides, fold muslin square in half from top to bottom and again from left to right.

**3.** Tie one end of string to pencil. Insert thumbtack through string 1" from pencil. Insert thumbtack through fabric as shown in **Fig. 1**; mark inside cutting line.

**Fig. 1**

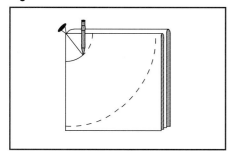

**4.** Repeat Step 3, inserting thumbtack 20¹/₂" from pencil; mark outside cutting line.

**5.** Cut along drawn lines through all fabric layers. For opening in back of skirt, cut through one layer of fabric along one fold line from outer to inner edge.

**6.** (**Note:** Refer to **Using Dimensional Paint**, page 106, for painting tips.) Paint decorative "stitches" along raw edges of fabric scraps; allow to dry.

**7.** Follow **Binding**, page 102, to add 2¹/₂"w fused binding along opening edges and inner edge of skirt.

**8.** Glue fringe along outer edge on right side of skirt, trimming to fit; allow to dry.

**9.** With ¹/₂" of ribbon extending beyond one opening edge of skirt, glue ribbon along top edge of fringe; trim remaining ribbon end ¹/₂" past remaining opening edge of skirt. Fold ribbon ends to wrong side of skirt and glue in place. Allow to dry.

# SANTA'S HOMESPUN TREE

*The ideal size for tabletop display, our wooden dowel tree is wrapped with strips of homespun fabric and hung with Santa, reindeer, and sleigh ornaments. The merry trimmers and radiant star topper are all fast and easy to make by fusing fabric and batting to a brown paper base.*

## Tree

**You will need:**
Wonder-Under® transfer web
6¹/₂" dia. clay pot for base
acrylic paint to coordinate with fabrics
36" length of ¹/₂" dia. dowel for tree trunk
one each 8", 12", 16", and 20" length of ¹/₄" dia. dowel for branches
homespun fabrics for tree and bow
corrugated cardboard
floral foam
brown paper raffia
brown paper bag for appliqué
fabric scrap for appliqué
7" square of cotton batting
twigs
paintbrush
fabric glue
hot glue gun and glue sticks
pressing cloth

**1.** Use acrylic paint to paint pot; allow to dry.

**2.** Measure around pot rim. Cut a strip of cardboard 1¹/₄"w by the determined measurement and tear a strip of fabric ³/₄"w by the determined measurement. Use fabric glue to glue fabric strip to center of cardboard; allow to dry. Hot glue cardboard around pot rim.

**3.** Tear several 1" x 24" fabric strips. Tie strips into a bow. Hot glue bow over ends of cardboard and fabric strip.

**4.** To cover tree trunk, tear a 1" x 18" strip from one fabric. Beginning 11" from one end of ¹/₂" dia. dowel and keeping edges of strip even while wrapping, wrap strip around dowel. Use fabric glue to glue end to secure and allow to dry. Repeat to cover dowel using assorted fabrics.

**5.** Follow Step 4 to cover ¹/₄" dia. dowel lengths. Referring to **Fig. 1** for branch placement and wrapping in a crisscross direction, use strips to secure branches to trunk. Use fabric glue to secure ends of strips; allow to dry.

**Fig. 1**

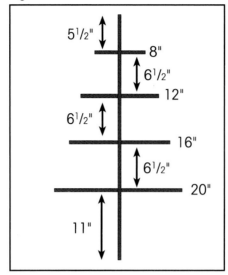

**6.** Fill pot with floral foam, trimming to fit. Insert bottom end of tree trunk into center of foam block. Cover foam with raffia.

**7.** Using patterns, page 116, follow **Making Appliqués**, page 102, to make one star A appliqué from paper bag and one star B appliqué from fabric scrap.

**8.** Center and fuse star A appliqué to batting. Center and fuse star B appliqué to star A.

**9.** Trim batting to ¹/₄" around appliqué.

**10.** Hot glue twigs to back of star.

**11.** Hot glue star to top of tree.

## Santa Ornaments

**Note:** Supplies are for making one ornament.

**You will need:**
Wonder-Under® transfer web
brown paper bag
assorted fabrics for appliqués
cotton batting scrap for appliqués
4" x 5¹/₂" piece of cotton batting
two artificial red berries
6" length of string
red crayon
black permanent pen
large-eye needle
hot glue gun and glue sticks
pressing cloth

**1.** Using patterns, page 117, follow **Making Appliqués**, page 102, to make two (one in reverse) each of Santa base appliqués from paper bag; hat trim, eyebrow A, eyebrow B, and beard from batting; and hat, suit, and boots appliqués from fabrics.

**2.** Center and fuse one Santa base to batting. Arrange one set of appliqués on Santa base, overlapping as necessary; fuse in place.

**3.** Trim batting to ¹/₈" around appliqués.

**4.** Using remaining appliqués, repeat Step 2 on reverse side of ornament.

**5.** For face on each side of ornament, use permanent pen to add eyes and crayon to add cheeks. Glue berry to face for nose.

**6.** For hanger, thread needle with string; pull string through top of ornament and knot ends together.

## Reindeer Ornaments

**Note:** Supplies are for making one ornament.

**You will need:**
Wonder-Under® transfer web
brown paper bag
assorted fabrics for appliqués
4" x 5" piece of cotton batting
twigs for antlers
6" length of string
red and black permanent pens
large-eye needle
hot glue gun and glue sticks
pressing cloth

**1.** Using patterns, page 116, follow **Making Appliqués**, page 102, to make two (one in reverse) each of reindeer body base and reindeer head base appliqués from paper bag and ear A, ear B, hoof A, hoof B, and nose appliqués from fabrics.

**2.** Center and fuse one reindeer body base and each reindeer head base to batting. Trim batting to ¹/₈" around appliqués.

**3.** Arrange one set of appliqués on one side of reindeer body base and each reindeer head base; fuse in place. Arrange remaining appliqués on reverse side of reindeer body; fuse in place.

**4.** Glue twigs to back of one head for antlers. Glue one reindeer head to each side of reindeer body.

**5.** Use permanent pens to add face and body details on each side of ornament.

**6.** For hanger, thread needle with string; pull string through top of ornament and knot ends together.

## Sleigh Ornaments

**Note:** Supplies are for making one ornament.

> **You will need:**
> Wonder-Under® transfer web
> brown paper bag
> fabric scraps
> 4" x 6" piece of cotton batting
> large-eye needle
> 6" length of string
> red and green $1/16$"w satin ribbon
> two 6mm jingle bells
> hot glue gun and glue sticks
> pressing cloth

**1.** Using patterns, page 116, follow **Making Appliqués**, page 102, to make two (one in reverse) each of sleigh base appliqué from paper bag and sleigh and runner appliqués from fabric scraps.

**2.** Center and fuse one sleigh base to batting. Arrange one set of appliqués on sleigh base, overlapping as necessary; fuse in place.

**3.** Trim batting to $1/8$" around appliqués.

**4.** Using remaining appliqués, repeat Step 2 on reverse side of ornament.

**5.** Cut one 7" length each from red and green ribbon. Tie lengths into a bow; glue to sleigh. Glue bell to knot of bow. Repeat for reverse side of ornament.

**6.** For hanger, thread needle with string; pull string through top of ornament and knot ends together.

# QUILTER'S TREE SKIRT

*Bordered with old-time fabric yo-yos, this colorful tree skirt is a quilter's dream! The pieced project is sewn with homey fabrics for a charming look that never goes out of style.*

> **You will need:**
> 1 yd of 44/45"w fabric for border
> $3/8$ yd each of six 44/45"w fabrics for pieced circle
> 50" square of fabric (pieced as necessary) for backing
> fabric for binding
> assorted fabrics for yo-yos
> twenty-four $1/2$" to $5/8$" dia. buttons for yo-yos
> string
> thread to match fabrics
> compass
> thumbtack
> pencil
> tracing paper

**1.** Matching grey lines and arrows, trace panel A and panel B patterns, page 143, onto tracing paper. Use pattern to cut four pieces from each of six fabrics.

**2.** (**Note:** For all sewing steps, match right sides and raw edges and use a $1/4$" seam allowance, unless otherwise indicated.) Sew two pieces together along one long straight edge. Repeat to attach remaining pieces, leaving first and last pieces unsewn for tree skirt opening. Press seam allowances to one side.

**3.** For border pattern, cut a 27" square from tracing paper (pieced as necessary). Follow Steps 3 and 4 of **Crazy-Quilt Skirt**, page 31, inserting thumbtack $19^{1}/_{2}$" from pencil for inside cutting line and $25^{1}/_{2}$" from pencil for outside cutting line. Cut along drawn lines.

**4.** Use border pattern to cut four pieces from border fabric. Sewing along short edges, refer to Step 2 to sew pieces together.

**5.** Sew border to circle, easing as necessary. Clip seam allowance and press to one side. Trim any overlap at opening.

**6.** Using skirt top as a pattern, cut a piece from backing fabric. Matching wrong sides, baste skirt top and backing fabric together along all edges.

**7.** Machine stitch along seam between pieced circle and border.

**8.** Follow **Binding**, page 102, to add $2^{1}/_{2}$"w sewn binding to all raw edges of skirt.

**9.** For yo-yo pattern, use compass to draw a 5" dia. circle on tracing paper. For each yo-yo, use pattern and cut one circle from fabric. Turn raw edge of circle $1/4$" to wrong side. Using a double strand of thread, work a small **Running Stitch**, page 105, along turned edge. Pull ends of thread to tightly gather circle; knot thread and trim ends. With circle flattened and gathers at center, sew a button over opening. Repeat to make a total of 24 yo-yos.

**10.** Spacing yo-yos approximately 3" apart, hand sew edges of yo-yos to tree skirt border.

# COUNTRY ANGEL TREE TOPPER

*Bearing a basket of Christmas goodies and a tiny feather tree, our darling treetop angel is happy to help you celebrate the spirit of the season. The country cutie is crafted over a two-liter soda bottle and dressed in homespun fabrics for a sweet down-home look.*

## You will need:

Wonder-Under® transfer web
Wonder-Under® fusible tape
2-liter soda bottle
fabrics for clothing (see **Table**)
8" x 12" piece of muslin for legs
7" x 9" crocheted doily with rounded corners
2¹/₂" dia. pâpier-maché ball
braided doll hair
red, green, black, flesh, pink, and gold acrylic paints
two 13mm x 21mm oval wooden beads
twelve ¹/₄" dia. red wooden beads
fabric stiffener
4"h basket (including handle)
assorted dried flowers and greenery
small cinnamon sticks
small sprig of holly leaves with berries
miniature wired greenery for tree
floral foam to fit in basket
brown floral tape
1¹/₄"h wooden spool
1"w wooden star
7³/₄" length of ¹/₄" dia. dowel
assorted small buttons
jute twine
¹/₈" dia. paper wire
black permanent pen
polyester fiberfill
liner and flat paintbrushes
large-eye needle
quilting thread
wire cutters
ruler
tracing paper
hot glue gun and glue sticks
pressing cloth

**Note:** For all sewing steps, match right sides and raw edges and use a ¹/₄" seam allowance.

**1.** Mark bottle 4³/₄" from bottom; cut along drawn line.

**2.** For head, glue pâpier-maché ball to top of bottle. For hands and arms, cut a 15" length of paper wire; glue one oval wooden bead to each end of wire.

Paint head and hands flesh, cheeks pink, and eyes black; allow to dry.

**3.** Cut a 4" length of doll hair; tie with thread at center. Unbraid and fluff hair. Glue hair to top of head. Glue one holly sprig over thread.

**4.** Refer to **Table** to cut fabric pieces for clothing.

**5.** Follow **Fusing Basics**, page 102, to press fusible tape to right side of one short edge of dress fabric piece. Remove paper backing. Matching right sides and short edges, fuse edges together. Turn tube right side out. Use pen to draw "stitches" along one edge (bottom) of dress.

**6.** Baste ⁵/₈" from top edge of dress. Place dress over bottle. Pull thread, gathering dress to fit around neck of bottle.

**7.** For sleeves, repeat Step 5, fusing long edges of sleeve fabric piece together.

**8.** Insert arm wire into sleeves. Cut two 5" lengths of jute. Knot one length around each wrist. Center and glue arms to back of body 1" below neck. Bend arms to front of body.

**9.** For apron front, fuse web to fabric squares for patches; fuse patches to one piece of apron fabric. Use pen to draw "stitches" on each patch.

**10.** Cut two 12" lengths of jute. Use needle and jute to work a **Running Stitch**, page 105, ³/₈" from top edge of apron front. Repeat for apron back. Pull jute to gather. Arrange apron over dress, adjusting gathers as necessary. Tie apron front to apron back at shoulders. Fringe bottom of apron.

**11.** Tie ¹/₂" x 8" strip of fabric into a bow; sew button to center of bow. Glue bow to neck of dress.

**12.** Trace leg pattern, page 118, onto tracing paper. Follow **Sewing Shapes**, page 105, to make two legs from muslin piece. Stuff legs with fiberfill to 1" from top. Use black paint to paint shoes on legs; allow to dry. Use pen to draw laces. Glue legs to front of bottle.

**13.** For wings, baste across center of doily from top to bottom.

**14.** Pull basting thread to gather doily to shape wings; tie thread tightly to hold shape. Follow manufacturer's instructions to apply stiffener to wings; allow to dry. Clip basting threads.

**15.** Glue wings to back of angel.

**16.** For tree, wrap dowel length with floral tape. Use wire cutters to cut three 1¹/₂", four 2", and five 2¹/₂" lengths of greenery. Remove bottom ¹/₂" of greenery from each branch; bend exposed wire to a 90° angle.

**17.** Beginning 1¹/₂" from top of dowel, glue 1¹/₂" branches evenly around dowel. Repeat to add 2" branches, then 2¹/₂" branches 1¹/₂" below each layer of branches. Wrap dowel with floral tape again, covering ends of branches.

**18.** Paint star gold and spool red and green; allow to dry. Glue star to top of tree. Glue tree in hole of spool. Glue red beads to ends of branches.

**19.** Tie a loop of quilting thread through each button. Hang buttons on tree.

**20.** Place floral foam in basket. Arrange dried flowers, greenery, and cinnamon sticks in basket, gluing to secure.

**21.** Place tree on one side of angel and basket on opposite side. Bend arms to hold tree and basket.

| TABLE | |
|---|---|
| **Piece** | **Size (width x length)** |
| dress | 9¹/₂" x 29" (torn) |
| sleeves | 7" x 15" (torn) |
| apron | two 7" x 9¹/₂" (torn) |
| bow | ¹/₂" x 8" (torn) |
| patches | two 1" squares |

# PATCHWORK TREE SKIRT

*Christmas decorations crafted from homespun cloth, old-timey ticking, and vintage buttons not only show your love for the Yuletide but for country living as well. This cozy quilted tree skirt showcases a traditional pieced star pattern and fused-on Christmas tree appliqués.*

**You will need:**
Wonder-Under® transfer web
1 3/4 yds of 44/45"w green striped fabric
1 yd of 44/45"w green print fabric
1/2 yd of 44/45"w red print fabric
1/2 yd of 44/45"w red and black checked fabric
1 5/8 yds of 60"w fabric for backing
assorted fabrics for appliqués
54" square of low-loft polyester bonded batting
gold and green embroidery floss
52 assorted buttons
removable fabric marking pen
permanent pen
clear nylon thread
1" long safety pins
template material
tracing paper
pressing cloth

**Note:** For all sewing steps, match right sides, raw edges, and seams. Use a 1/4" seam allowance, unless otherwise indicated. Press seam allowances toward darker fabric whenever possible.

**1.** Wash and dry fabrics without using fabric softener; press.

**2.** Using patterns, pages 117 and 119, follow **Tracing Patterns**, page 105, to trace A, B, and C templates onto template material; cut out.

**3.** Matching grey lines and arrows, trace D template, pages 117 and 118, onto template material and E template, pages 119 and 120, onto tracing paper; cut out.

**4.** Using E pattern, made in Step 3, and F pattern, page 118, follow **Tracing Patterns** to trace one each full-size E and F templates onto template material.

**5.** Placing templates on straight grain of fabric, use removable pen to trace sixteen A's on red print fabric, 32 B's on green striped fabric, sixteen C's on red print fabric, eight D's on green striped fabric, eight E's on green striped fabric, and eight F's on green print fabric; cut out pieces.

**6.** Cut four 9" squares and four 4 3/4" squares from red and black checked fabric.

**7.** For each star block, refer to **Fig. 1** to sew one A, two B's, and two C's together to make **Row 1**. Sew two A's, four B's, and one 4 3/4" square together to make **Row 2**. Sew one A, two B's, and two C's together to make **Row 3**. Sew rows together to complete star block. Repeat to make four star blocks.

**Fig. 1**

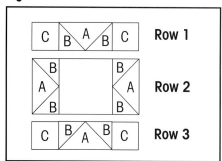

**8.** Refer to **Fig. 2a** to sew one D, one E, two F's and one 9" square together to make **Unit 1**. Refer to **Fig. 2b** to sew one D, one E, and one star block together to make **Unit 2**. Repeat to make four **Unit 1's** and four **Unit 2's**.

**Fig. 2a**

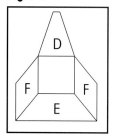

**Unit 1** (make 4)

**Fig. 2b**

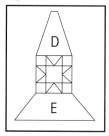

**Unit 2** (make 4)

**9.** To complete tree skirt top, refer to **Diagram** to sew **Unit 1's** and **Unit 2's** together, leaving first and last pieces unsewn for tree skirt opening.

**Diagram**

**10.** Using patterns, page 119, follow **Making Appliqués**, page 102, to make four each of tree and tree trunk appliqués and 28 star appliqués.

**11.** Arrange appliqués on tree skirt; fuse in place.

**12.** Place backing fabric, right side up, on batting. Matching right sides, place tree skirt top on backing; pin layers together. Using tree skirt top as pattern, trim batting and backing even with raw edges of tree skirt top.

**13.** Leaving an opening for turning, sew all layers together along all raw edges. Clip curves and turn right side out; press. Sew final closure by hand.

**14.** Beginning at outer edge and working toward center, baste all layers together.

**15.** Using clear thread, sew along each seamline, stitching through all layers.

**16.** Use three strands of green floss to work **Running Stitch**, page 105, around each star appliqué. Use four strands of gold floss to work **Running Stitch** around each tree appliqué and along inside edges of each tree block and center square of each star block.

**17.** Sew one button to each star and corners of each tree block and star block.

# APPLIQUÉD ORNAMENTS

*Cut in traditional shapes, these appliquéd ornaments look great on packages and wreaths, as well as on the tree! Make the soft charmers with a variety of Christmas prints fused to fleece.*

## Cardinal Ornament

**You will need:**
Wonder-Under® transfer web
two 5" squares of red print fabric
5" square of white fleece
tan fabric for beak appliqué
black embroidery floss
thread to match fabrics
9" length of jute twine
removable fabric marking pen
tracing paper
pressing cloth

**1.** Follow **Fusing Basics**, page 102, to fuse one 5" fabric square to each side of fleece.

**2.** Trace entire cardinal pattern, page 120, onto tracing paper; cut out. Use removable pen to trace around pattern and mark detail lines on one side of fused square.

**3.** Using pattern, page 120, follow **Making Appliqués**, page 102, to make one beak appliqué in reverse. Arrange appliqué on marked side of square; fuse in place.

**4.** Using thread to coordinate with fabrics and a medium-width zigzag stitch with a very short stitch length, stitch around all edges of cardinal and appliqué and over detail lines.

**5.** Cutting just outside outer edge of zigzag stitching, trim away excess fabric.

**6.** Use six strands of embroidery floss to work a **French Knot**, page 105, for eye.

**7.** For hanger, fold jute in half and knot ends together. Tack knot to back of ornament.

## Bell Ornament

**You will need:**
Wonder-Under® transfer web
two 5" squares of tan fabric
5" square of white fleece
green fabric for band and clapper appliqués
thread to match fabrics
9" length of jute twine
removable fabric marking pen
tracing paper
pressing cloth

**1.** Follow **Fusing Basics**, page 102, to fuse one 5" fabric square to each side of fleece.

**2.** Trace entire bell pattern, page 120, onto tracing paper; cut out. Use removable pen to trace around pattern and mark detail lines on one side of fused square.

**3.** Using patterns, page 120, follow **Making Appliqués**, page 102, to make one each of band and clapper appliqués in reverse. Arrange appliqués on marked side of square; fuse in place.

**4.** Using thread to coordinate with fabrics and a medium-width zigzag stitch with a very short stitch length, stitch around all edges of bell and appliqués and over detail lines.

**5.** Cutting just outside outer edge of zigzag stitching, trim away excess fabric.

**6.** Follow Step 7 of **Cardinal Ornament** instructions for hanger.

## Tree Ornament

**You will need:**
Wonder-Under® transfer web
two 6" squares of green fabric
6" square of white fleece
brown fabric for tree trunk appliqué
nine 5mm beads
thread to match fabrics
removable fabric marking pen
9" length of jute twine
tracing paper
pressing cloth

**1.** Follow **Fusing Basics**, page 102, to fuse one 6" fabric square to each side of fleece.

**2.** Trace entire tree pattern, page 120, onto tracing paper; cut out. Use removable pen to trace around pattern and mark detail lines on one side of fused square.

**3.** Using pattern, page 120, follow **Making Appliqués**, page 102, to make one tree trunk appliqué in reverse. Arrange appliqué on marked side of square; fuse in place.

**4.** Using thread to coordinate with fabrics and a medium-width zigzag stitch with a very short stitch length, stitch around all edges of tree and appliqué and over detail lines.

**5.** Cutting just outside outer edge of zigzag stitching, trim away excess fabric.

**6.** Sew beads to ornament as desired.

**7.** Follow Step 7 of **Cardinal Ornament** instructions for hanger.

## Church Ornament

**You will need:**
Wonder-Under® transfer web
two 6" squares of cream fabric
6" square of white fleece
red fabric for steeple and roof appliqués
tan fabric for door and window appliqués
removable fabric marking pen
thread to match fabrics
9" length of jute twine
tracing paper
pressing cloth

**1.** Follow **Fusing Basics**, page 102, to fuse one 6" fabric square to each side of fleece.

**2.** Trace entire church pattern, page 120, onto tracing paper; cut out. Use removable pen to trace around pattern and mark detail line on one side of fused square.

**3.** Using patterns, page 120, follow **Making Appliqués**, page 102, to make two large window appliqués and one each of steeple, roof, door, and small window appliqués in reverse. Arrange appliqués on marked side of square; fuse in place.

**4.** Using thread to coordinate with fabrics and a medium-width zigzag stitch with a very short stitch length, stitch around all edges of church and appliqués and over detail line.

**5.** Cutting just outside outer edge of zigzag stitching, trim away excess fabric.

**6.** Follow Step 7 of **Cardinal Ornament** instructions for hanger.

# FOUR SEASONS SNOWMEN

*Dressed up with simple accents, these whimsical snowmen welcome each season with open arms. They're sure to become year-round conversation pieces, whether you display them one by one or as a set. They'll make a perfect addition to a friend's snowman collection, too!*

## Basic Snowman

**You will need:**
two 6$\frac{1}{2}$" x 10" pieces of quilted mattress cover **or** muslin
polyester fiberfill
dried beans
instant coffee
two 4" long twigs
round toothpick
orange and black acrylic paint
small paintbrush
seam ripper
tapestry needle
tracing paper
fabric glue
hot glue gun and glue sticks

**1.** Dissolve two tablespoons instant coffee in two cups hot water; allow to cool. Soak mattress cover pieces in coffee several minutes; remove from coffee. Allow to dry and press.

**2.** Trace snowman pattern, page 121, onto tracing paper; cut out. Follow **Sewing Shapes**, page 105, to make one snowman from mattress cover pieces.

**3.** Stuff snowman with fiberfill to within 1$\frac{1}{2}$" of opening. Fill remaining 1$\frac{1}{2}$" with dried beans. Sew final closure by hand.

**4.** For arms, use seam ripper to open a small hole in each side seam. Pull a small amount of fiberfill through hole. Hot glue one twig in each hole.

**5.** Use black paint to paint dots for eyes and mouth; allow to dry.

**6.** For nose, paint toothpick orange; allow to dry. Cut $\frac{3}{4}$" from one end of toothpick. Apply a small amount of fabric glue to $\frac{1}{2}$" of cut end of nose. Insert tapestry needle through back of head to front, making a guide hole. Insert cut end of toothpick through guide hole, stopping when nose is desired length. Allow to dry.

## Spring Snowman

**You will need:**
basic snowman
1" square of red fabric
3" square of blue fabric
$\frac{3}{4}$" x 12" torn strip of blue fabric
$\frac{3}{8}$" x 2" torn strip of green fabric
blue and black embroidery floss
two $\frac{3}{4}$" dia. shank buttons for earmuffs
$\frac{1}{2}$" dia. blue button
$\frac{1}{2}$" dia. black button
4" length of 16 gauge wire
wire cutters
3" length of jute twine
Spanish moss
tracing paper
hot glue gun and glue sticks

**1.** For earmuffs, bend wire in a semicircle. Glue to head of snowman. Use wire cutters to remove shank from $\frac{3}{4}$" dia. buttons. Glue one button to each end of wire on head.

**2.** For birdhouse pole, tack top and bottom ends of jute to front of snowman.

**3.** Trace birdhouse and heart patterns, page 121, onto tracing paper. Use patterns to cut one birdhouse from blue fabric and one heart from red fabric.

**4.** Using one strand of black floss and **Running Stitch**, page 105, stitch heart to birdhouse and birdhouse to snowman.

**5.** Glue a small amount of moss to birdhouse and to bottom of pole.

**6.** Thread six strands of matching floss through black and blue buttons; tie ends at front of button. Glue black button to birdhouse over moss and blue button to snowman.

**7.** Tie green fabric strip to pole.

**8.** For scarf, tie remaining fabric strip around neck.

## Summer Snowman

**You will need:**
basic snowman
1$\frac{3}{8}$" x 1$\frac{3}{4}$" piece of white fabric
1$\frac{3}{4}$" x 2" piece of red fabric
$\frac{5}{8}$" x 12" torn strip of green fabric
two $\frac{3}{8}$" x 2" torn strips of green fabric
tan, red, and black embroidery floss
1$\frac{1}{2}$" length of 16 gauge wire
$\frac{1}{2}$" dia. red button
$\frac{5}{8}$" dia. red button
two $\frac{1}{2}$" dia. tan buttons
2" length of jute twine
Spanish moss
hot glue gun and glue sticks

**1.** Tack jute to front of snowman. Glue a small amount of moss to bottom of jute.

**2.** For seed packet, center white fabric piece on red fabric piece. Using one strand of black embroidery floss and **Straight Stitch**, page 105, stitch the word "SEEDS" along top of seed packet. Use **Running Stitch**, page 105, to sew seed packet to snowman over top end of jute.

**3.** For flower on seed packet, sew $\frac{5}{8}$" dia. button to center of seed packet. Use two strands of black floss to stitch a long **Straight Stitch** for stem. For leaves, tie a knot at center of one 2" long green fabric strip and glue to bottom of stem.

**4.** For flower in hand, knot six strands of red floss through holes of $\frac{1}{2}$" dia. button. Glue one end of wire length to back of button. Tie remaining 2" long fabric strip below button. Glue flower to end of one arm.

**5.** For scarf, tie 12" long fabric strip around neck.

**6.** Using six strands of tan floss, sew tan buttons to snowman, tying ends at front of buttons.

# Autumn Snowman

**You will need:**
basic snowman
3¹/₄" x 2¹/₄" piece of rust fabric
3¹/₄" x 2¹/₄" piece of batting
³/₄" x 12" torn strip of brown fabric
³/₈" x 2" torn strip of green fabric
green and black embroidery floss
3" dia. straw hat
crow-shaped button
two ¹/₂" dia. wooden buttons
1" length of jute twine
Spanish moss
tracing paper
hot glue gun and glue sticks

**1.** Use four strands of black floss to sew crow button to hat. Glue moss to inside edge of hat under crow. Glue hat to snowman.

**2.** For scarf, tie brown fabric strip around neck, catching a small amount of moss in knot.

**3.** Trace pumpkin pattern, page 121, onto tracing paper; cut out. Use pattern to cut one pumpkin each from rust fabric and batting.

**4.** Layering fabric on batting, use **Running Stitch**, page 105, and one strand of black floss to attach pumpkin to snowman and stitch detail lines.

**5.** For stem, tack one end of jute at top of pumpkin. Fray end and trim as desired. Tie a knot in remaining fabric strip and glue to pumpkin. Glue moss below pumpkin.

**6.** Using six strands of green floss, sew buttons to snowman, tying ends at front of buttons.

## Winter Snowman

**You will need:**
basic snowman
2¹/₂" dia. black felt hat
¹/₂" x 12" torn strip of red fabric
five assorted ¹/₂"w torn strips of green fabric in 1¹/₄", 1¹/₂", 1³/₄", 2¹/₂", and 3" lengths
³/₈" x 2" torn strip of green fabric
red embroidery floss
two ¹/₂" dia. black buttons
four ³/₈" dia. white buttons
¹/₂" dia. white button
3¹/₂" length of jute twine
hot glue gun and glue sticks

**1.** For tree trunk, tack jute vertically to front of snowman.

**2.** Using floss, sew ¹/₂" dia. button to center of 3" long green fabric strip. Sew a ³/₈" dia. button to center of each remaining ¹/₂"w green fabric strip. Glue strips to jute for tree branches.

**3.** For hat decoration, tie a knot in center of ³/₈" x 2" green fabric strip. Tack to hat. Using six strands of floss, work three **French Knots**, page 105, on hat for berries. Glue hat to snowman.

**4.** For scarf, tie red fabric strip around neck.

**5.** Using six strands of floss, sew black buttons to snowman, tying ends at front of buttons.

# COZY TREE-TRIMMERS

*Christmas trees, cozy mittens, and gingerbread men always kindle thoughts of the holiday season. Finished with blanket stitch embroidery and accented with buttons, these quick-to-make woolen ornaments will bring country warmth and good cheer to all!*

## Gingerbread Man Ornament

**You will need:**
Heavy Duty Wonder-Under® transfer web
two 5" squares of tan wool fabric
5" square of fleece
white, red, and green embroidery floss
two buttons
removable fabric marking pen
embroidery needle
6" length of clear nylon thread
tracing paper
pressing cloth

**1.** Follow **Fusing Basics**, page 102, to fuse one tan fabric square to each side of fleece.

**2.** Trace gingerbread man pattern, page 121, onto tracing paper; cut out. Use removable pen to trace around pattern on one side of fused square. Cut out gingerbread man along drawn line.

**3.** Use six strands of green floss to work a **French Knot**, page 105, for each eye. Use six strands of white floss to work **Blanket Stitch**, page 104, around outer edge of ornament.

**4.** Using twelve strands of red floss and sewing through top layer of ornament only, sew buttons to ornament, tying ends at front of buttons.

**5.** For hanger, use needle to pull clear thread through top center of ornament; knot ends together.

## Tree Ornament

**You will need:**
Heavy Duty Wonder-Under® transfer web
two 5" squares of green wool fabric
5" square of fleece
tan wool fabric for tree trunk appliqué
red embroidery floss
four buttons
removable fabric marking pen
embroidery needle
6" length of clear nylon thread
tracing paper
pressing cloth

**1.** Follow **Fusing Basics**, page 102, to fuse one green fabric square to each side of fleece.

**2.** Trace tree pattern, page 121, onto tracing paper; cut out. Use removable pen to trace around pattern on one side of fused square. Cut out tree along drawn line.

**3.** Using patterns, page 121, follow **Making Appliqués**, page 102, to make one tree trunk appliqué from tan fabric. Arrange appliqué on one side of tree; fuse in place.

**4.** Use six strands of floss to work **Blanket Stitch**, page 104, around edges of tree and tree trunk.

**5.** Follow Step 4 of **Gingerbread Man** instructions to attach buttons.

**6.** Follow Step 5 of **Gingerbread Man** instructions for hanger.

## Mitten Ornament

**You will need:**
Heavy Duty Wonder-Under® transfer web
two 5" squares of red wool fabric
5" square of fleece
tan wool fabric for star appliqué
blue embroidery floss
button
removable fabric marking pen
embroidery needle
6" length of clear nylon thread
tracing paper
pressing cloth

**1.** Follow **Fusing Basics**, page 102, to fuse one red fabric square to each side of fleece.

**2.** Trace mitten pattern, page 121, onto tracing paper; cut out. Use removable pen to trace around pattern on one side of fused square. Cut out mitten along drawn line.

**3.** Using patterns, page 121, follow **Making Appliqués**, page 102, to make one star appliqué from tan fabric. Arrange appliqué on one side of mitten; fuse in place.

**4.** Use six strands of floss to work **Blanket Stitch**, page 104, around edges of mitten and star.

**5.** Follow Step 4 of **Gingerbread Man** instructions to attach button.

**6.** Follow Step 5 of **Gingerbread Man** instructions for hanger.

# deck the halls

**T**oday, holiday decorating includes far more than a string of cheery lights and a gaily trimmed tree. Our Christmas spirit begins outdoors with a bright mailbox banner and flag to greet those who come to call. The cordial mood continues inside, where we place favorite Yuletide touches — such as quilted wall hangings, patchwork stockings, and a stuffed snowman — to warm every nook and cranny. This collection presents lots of choices to help deck the halls in festive fashion!

# QUILTER'S CHRISTMAS WALL HANGING

*For this wonderful wall hanging, we used a variety of fast techniques, such as fusing on our triangle-squares and machine appliquéing with clear nylon thread. Finished with fused-on shapes and permanent-pen "stitches," our heartfelt sentiments will spread wishes of "piece" and joy to all your Yuletide guests!*

## You will need:

Wonder-Under® transfer web
fabrics for piecing wall hanging front (see **Table**)
assorted fabrics for appliqués
29" x 30" piece each of fabric for backing and low-loft polyester bonded batting
7" x 26" strip of fabric for hanging sleeve
3" x 7" rectangle of white print fabric for mini-quilts
3" x 7" rectangle of batting for mini-quilts
fabric for binding
tear-away stabilizer
12" length of jute twine
clear nylon thread
black and pink permanent pens
fabric marking pencil
1" long safety pins for basting
pressing cloth

## PIECING WALL HANGING TOP

**1.** Wash, dry, and press fabrics.

**2.** Refer to **Table** to cut fabrics for piecing wall hanging front.

**3.** (**Note:** For all sewing steps, match right sides and raw edges of fabrics, use a ¹/₄" seam allowance, and press seam allowances to one side. Refer to **Assembly Diagram** and **Unit Key** for piece placement.) Sew one A and one B together; repeat to make six AB's. Sew two AB's, C, D, E, and F together to make **Unit 1**. Sew I, four G's, and three H's together to make **Unit 2**. Sew K and three J's together to make **Unit 3**. Sew four AB's, three L's, three M's, and four N's, together to make **Unit 4**.

**4.** Sew **Unit 1**, **Unit 2**, **Unit 3**, then **Unit 4** together to make center section of wall hanging top.

**5.** Sew one O to each end of each P to make two OP's. Sew Q's, then OP's to center section to complete wall hanging top.

**6.** Using patterns, pages 122 and 123, follow **Making Appliqués**, page 102, to make one each of large tree, grass, face, beard, mustache, cap, cap trim, coat, and coat trim appliqués; two medium tree appliqués; two (one in reverse) each of glove, boot, and cuff trim appliqués; three each of square A, large heart, small tree, and tree trunk appliqués; four each of friendship star and star A appliqués; five star B appliqués; seven (three white and four red) small heart appliqués; and twelve triangle A appliqués.

**7.** Arrange appliqués on wall hanging top, overlapping as necessary; fuse in place.

**8.** Use clear thread and follow **Machine Appliqué**, page 105, to stitch over raw edges of appliqués.

**9.** Use pens to draw eyes and nose on face; "stitches" along edges of beard, mustache, and small hearts in **Unit 3**; and write "Joy," "Piece," and "Quilt" on small hearts in **Unit 3**.

## QUILTING WALL HANGING

**1.** Using **Quilting Diagram** as a suggestion, use fabric marking pencil to mark wall hanging top.

**2.** Place backing fabric wrong side up. Place batting on backing. Center wall hanging top, right side up, on batting. Working from center outward, use safety pins to baste layers together, placing pins 3" to 4" apart.

**3.** Machine stitch along marked lines.

## FINISHING WALL HANGING

**1.** To make mini-quilts, fuse white print rectangle to batting rectangle. Cut out three 2" squares. Referring to **Mini-Quilt Diagram** and using patterns, follow **Making Appliqués** to make one each of square B and rectangle appliqués, three triangle B appliqués, and four each of arrowhead and triangle C appliqués. Arrange appliqués on squares; fuse in place. Use black pen to draw "stitches" around outer edge and around each appliqué on each mini-quilt. Tack mini-quilts to jute. Tack ends of jute to Santa's gloves.

**2.** Follow **Binding**, page 102, to add 2¹/₂"w sewn binding to wall hanging.

**3.** For hanging sleeve, press short edges of strip ¹/₄" to wrong side; press ¹/₄" to wrong side again. Stitch along first fold. Matching right sides and long edges, stitch ¹/₄" from long edges to form a tube. Turn right side out and press. Center and pin sleeve to quilt back 1" below top edge. Hand sew both long edges to quilt back, taking care not to stitch through front of quilt.

### Mini-Quilt Diagram

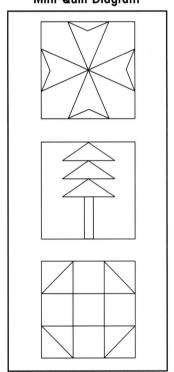

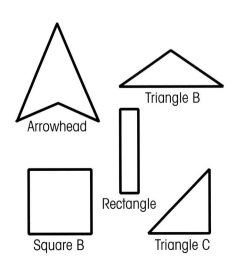

Arrowhead

Triangle B

Rectangle

Square B

Triangle C

| TABLE | | |
|---|---|---|
| Piece | Size (width x length) | Number - Fabric |
| A | 2" x 3½" | cut six - green print |
| B | 2" x 3½" | cut one - red plaid |
| C | 6½" x 8½" | cut one - tan print |
| D | 1½" x 6½" | cut one - red plaid |
| E | 1½" x 12½" | cut one - red plaid |
| F | 11½" x 12½" | cut one - tan check |
| G | 3" x 3" | cut four - brown check |
| H | 3" x 3" | cut three - tan print |
| I | 1" x 3" | cut one - red plaid |
| J | 3½" x 3½" | cut three - two different red plaids |
| K | 3½" x 6" | cut one - cream plaid |
| L | 3½" x 3½" | cut three - cream plaid |
| M | 3½" x 3½" | cut three - brown check |
| N | 3½" x 3½" | cut four - tan print |
| O | 3½" x 3½" | cut four - red plaid |
| P | 3½" x 21½" | cut two - green check |
| Q | 3½" x 21" | cut two - green check |

**Assembly Diagram**

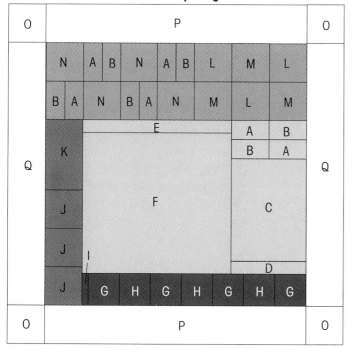

**Quilting Diagram**

**UNIT KEY**

- Unit 1  ▪ - Unit 3
▪ - Unit 2  ▪ - Unit 4

# ROLY-POLY STOCKING HANGERS

*Our adorable Santa and his frosty friend are just waiting to give you a hand with holding your Christmas stockings! The helpful duo is crafted by wrapping bricks with fabric or batting for the bodies, then adding heads and arms cut from cardboard and poster board.*

## Snowman Stocking Hanger

**You will need:**
cotton batting
3" x 24" piece of fabric for scarf
orange felt for nose
fabric for cheeks
11" x 14" piece of fusible interfacing
12" length of $1/2$"w grosgrain ribbon
black embroidery floss
pair of infant's black socks
one ladies' green sock
$2^1/2$"w x 8"l x 4"h brick
two black buttons for eyes
cardboard
poster board
black permanent pen
tracing paper
hot glue gun and glue sticks

**1.** Cut an 11" x 14" piece from batting. Follow manufacturer's instructions to fuse interfacing to one side of batting. Use interfaced batting to wrap brick package-style with seam at back; glue in place.

**2.** Using patterns, pages 123 and 124, trace head, body, and arm patterns onto tracing paper; cut out. Draw around head and body patterns on cardboard and arm pattern twice on poster board; cut out shapes.

**3.** Using patterns, cut one head, one body, and two arms from batting. Glue batting shapes to one side of cardboard and poster board shapes.

**4.** Using patterns and leaving at least 2" between shapes, draw around head and body once and arms twice on batting. Cut out shapes 1" outside drawn lines. Make clips in edges of batting to $1/8$" from drawn lines on each shape.

**5.** For head, center cardboard head, batting side down, on one side of batting shape. Alternating sides and pulling batting taut, glue clipped edges of batting to back of head. Repeat for body and arms.

**6.** Glue front of body to back of brick. Sew center of ribbon length to batting at center front of brick.

**7.** For each mitten, turn one black sock wrong side out; cut $2^1/2$" of ribbing from sock. Baste $1/4$" from raw edge of ribbing and pull thread to gather; knot ends together. Turn mitten right side out. Roll ribbed end of mitten to right side. Place mitten on rounded end of one arm; glue in place.

**8.** Overlapping and placing mittens over center of ribbon length on front of brick, wrap arms around brick; glue in place.

**9.** Trace cheek and nose patterns, page 123, onto tracing paper. Use patterns to cut two cheeks from fabric and one nose from felt. Use pen to draw "stitches" along edges of cheeks. Roll nose into a cone shape; glue to secure.

**10.** Sew buttons to head for eyes. Use three strands of black floss to work **Running Stitch**, page 105, for mouth. Glue cheeks and nose in place.

**11.** Glue back of head to front of body.

**12.** For hat, cut green sock at heel (**Fig. 1**). Turn sock piece to wrong side. Baste $1/4$" from raw edge of ribbing and pull thread to gather; knot ends together. Turn hat right side out. Roll ribbed end to right side. Stuff hat with a small amount of batting and place on head; glue in place.

**Fig. 1**

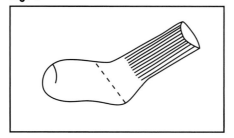

**13.** Make 1" cuts $1/8$" apart in short ends of fabric for scarf. Fold scarf in half lengthwise; wrap around head and shoulders.

**14.** To hang stocking, place loop of stocking between mittens; tie ribbon into a bow through loop.

## Santa Stocking Hanger

**You will need:**
fabric to cover brick, body, and arms
fabric to cover head
assorted fabrics for cheeks, star, and hat
11" x 14" piece of fusible fleece
cotton batting
12" length of $1/2$"w grosgrain ribbon
black embroidery floss
pair of infant's green socks
curly wool doll hair for beard
$2^1/2$"w x 8"l x 4"h brick
two black buttons for eyes
red shank-style button for nose
cardboard
poster board
black permanent pen
tracing paper
hot glue gun and glue sticks

**1.** Cut an 11" x 14" piece from fabric to cover brick. Follow manufacturer's instructions to fuse fleece to wrong side of fabric. With fleece side of fabric next to brick, wrap brick package-style with seam at back; glue in place.

**2.** Follow Steps 2 and 3 of **Snowman Stocking Hanger** instructions to trace patterns; cut out shapes from cardboard, poster board, and batting; and glue batting pieces to cardboard and poster board shapes.

**3.** Using patterns and leaving at least 2" between shapes, draw around head and body once and arms twice on fabric. Cut out shapes 1" outside drawn lines. Make clips in edges of fabric to $1/8$" from drawn lines on each shape.

**4.** For head, center cardboard head, batting side down, on wrong side of fabric shape. Alternating sides and pulling fabric taut, glue clipped edges of fabric to back of head. Repeat for body and arms.

50

**5.** Using green socks for mittens, follow Steps 6 - 8 of **Snowman Stocking Hanger** instructions to make Santa base.

**6.** Trace cheek and small star patterns, page 123, onto tracing paper. Use patterns to make two cheeks and one star from fabric. Use pen to draw "stitches" along edges of cheeks and star.

**7.** Sew black buttons to head for eyes. Glue red button to face for nose. Glue cheeks in place.

**8.** Glue back of head to front of body.

**9.** For beard, cut several 6" to 8" lengths of doll hair. Fold each length in half; glue fold to chin. Repeat to cover lower $1/3$ of face. For mustache, cut several 5" lengths of hair. Fold lengths in half; glue fold to face below nose. Arrange and trim beard and mustache as desired.

**10.** Follow **Tracing Patterns**, page 105, to trace hat and hat trim patterns, page 124, onto tracing paper. Use patterns to cut hat from fabric and hat trim from batting.

**11.** Matching raw edges, glue bottom curved edge of hat trim to wrong side of bottom edge of hat. Fold hat trim to right side; press. Use three strands of black floss to work **Running Stitch**, page 105, along top edge of hat trim.

**12.** Matching right sides and raw edges, fold hat in half; glue $1/4$" of edges together. Turn hat to right side.

**13.** Place hat on head; glue in place. Fold tip of hat to hat trim; glue in place. Glue star to tip of hat.

**14.** To hang stocking, place loop of stocking between mittens; tie ribbon into a bow through loop.

# CHRISTMAS CANDLES FLAG

*Light up your seasonal celebration with this colorful decorative flag! Intended for outdoor use, the festive banner features a trio of Christmas candles appliquéd onto both sides of the red nylon background.*

## You will need:
- 4⅝ yds of Heavy Duty Wonder-Under® transfer web
- 1⅝ yds of 44/45"w red nylon flag fabric for background and berries
- 1½ yds of 44/45"w white nylon flag fabric for candles
- ⅞ yd of 44/45"w green nylon flag fabric for leaves
- ½ yd of 44/45"w yellow nylon flag fabric for flames
- tear-away stabilizer
- two 1" long pieces of self-adhesive hook and loop fastener tape
- light tan thread for wicks
- thread to match fabrics
- fabric marking pencil
- tracing paper
- pressing cloth

## MAKING FLAG BACKGROUND

(**Note:** Instructions refer to side of flag with edges folded under as wrong side.)

**1.** Cut one 36" x 54" piece from red fabric. Fold two long edges and one short edge of background fabric under ½"; press. Fold under ½" again; press. Machine straight stitch close to first folds; stitch again close to outer edges.

**2.** For casing, fold remaining short edge ½" to wrong side; press. Fold 2½" to wrong side again; press and unfold. To prevent flag from sliding on flagpole, place loop side of hook and loop tape on wrong side of flag at second fold (**Fig. 1**). Machine straight stitch around edges of tape. Attach hook side of tape to pole.

**Fig. 1**

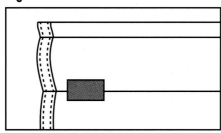

**3.** Refold fabric; sew close to first fold 2½" from top edge. Sew again 2⅛" from top edge to form a casing.

## APPLIQUÉING THE FLAG

**1.** Follow **Fusing Basics**, page 102, to press web to wrong side of white fabric. Do not remove paper backing. Cut two large candles 7½" x 31½" and four small candles 7½" x 25½" from fused fabric.

**2.** Using patterns, page 126, follow **Making Appliqués**, page 102, to make six (three in reverse) flame appliqués from yellow fabric, eight (four in reverse) leaf A appliqués from green fabric, and six berry appliqués from red fabric.

**3.** Referring to **Diagram**, arrange one set of appliqués on right side of flag, overlapping as necessary; fuse in place. Using edges of appliqués as a guide, carefully straight stitch along edge of each appliqué. Using stitching as a placement guide, arrange remaining set of appliqués on wrong side of flag, overlapping as necessary; fuse in place.

**4.** Use matching thread and a medium-width zigzag stitch with a very short stitch length to stitch over raw edges of appliqués.

**5.** For wicks, refer to **Diagram** and use fabric marking pencil and a ruler to draw a line on right side of flag from bottom center of each flame to top center of each candle. Cut three 1" x 3" pieces of stabilizer. Center one piece of stabilizer under each drawn line on wrong side of flag; pin in place. With presser foot centered on each drawn line and using light tan thread, stitch wicks using a medium-width zigzag stitch with a very short stitch length. Carefully tear away stabilizer.

**Diagram**

# MERRY MAILBOX BANNER

*Collecting the mail will be a special treat when you display this joyful mailbox cover. Appliquéd with a holly wreath, the weatherproof decoration offers passersby a cheery greeting.*

**You will need:**
Heavy Duty Wonder-Under® transfer web
1²/₃ yds of 44/45"w white nylon flag fabric for background
two 20" square pieces of dark green nylon flag fabric for wreath
³/₈ yd of 44/45"w green nylon flag fabric for leaves
¹/₂ yd of 44/45"w dia. red nylon flag fabric for bow
2 yds of tear-away stabilizer
eighteen ⁵/₈" dia. red shank buttons
four 1" square drapery weights with sewing tabs
removable fabric marking pen
string
thumbtack
seam ripper
thread to match fabrics
tracing paper
pencil
pressing cloth

**1.** Cut a 20¹/₂" x 60" piece of background fabric. Fold each long edge ¹/₂" to wrong side; press. Fold ¹/₂" to wrong side again; press. Machine stitch close to first folds; stitch again close to outer edges.

**2.** Fold each short edge 1" to wrong side; press. Fold 1" to wrong side again; press. Insert one weight in hem at each corner with tab extending above hemline. Machine stitch each edge close to first folds, catching tab in stitching.

**3.** Follow **Fusing Basics**, page 102, to press web to wrong side of one wreath fabric piece. Matching right sides, fold fabric piece in half from top to bottom and again from left to right.

**4.** Tie one end of string to pencil. Insert thumbtack through string at 3¹/₂" from pencil. Insert thumbtack through fabric as shown in **Fig. 1** and mark inside cutting line.

**Fig. 1**

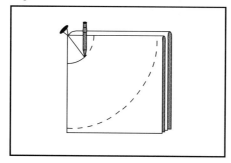

**5.** Repeat Step 4, inserting thumbtack 9" from pencil to mark outside cutting line.

**6.** Cut along drawn lines through all fabric layers. Unfold wreath.

**7.** Using remaining wreath fabric piece, repeat Steps 3 - 6 to make a second wreath.

**8.** Using patterns, page 127, follow **Making Appliqués**, page 102, to make 24 (ten in reverse) leaf B appliqués from green fabric, four (two in reverse) each of bow and streamer appliqués from red fabric, and two knot appliqués from red fabric.

**9.** Refer to **Diagram** to arrange one set of appliqués on each end of banner, overlapping as necessary; fuse in place.

**10.** Use matching thread and follow **Machine Appliqué**, page 105, to stitch over raw edges of appliqués and to add detail lines to bow and leaves.

**11.** Sew buttons to banner for berries.

**12.** For ties to anchor banner to mailbox, cut four 3" x 12¹/₂" strips of background fabric. Matching right sides and long edges, fold one strip in half. Using a ¹/₄" seam allowance, sew along long raw edge. Turn tie right side out; press. Sew short ends closed by hand. Repeat with remaining strips.

**13.** Pin one end of one tie to wrong side of banner 23" from one short edge and 4" from adjacent long edge. Sew ¹/₂" of inner end of tie in place (**Fig. 2**). Repeat for each remaining tie.

**Fig. 2**

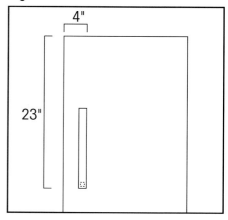

**14.** To make an opening for flag, place banner over mailbox with flag in down position. Use removable pen to mark a small dot at left end of flag arm. Measure horizontally 4" toward top of flag arm; mark point with a small dot. Use a ruler to draw a line between dots.

**15.** Using a narrow-width zigzag stitch with a very short stitch length, stitch on both sides of drawn line between dots. Use a wide-width zigzag stitch with a very short stitch length to tack each end of flag opening. Use seam ripper to cut an opening for flag along drawn line.

**Diagram**

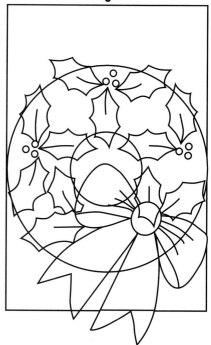

# AWAY IN A MANGER WALL HANGING

*An inspirational addition to your holiday decor, this charming wall quilt portrays a host of angels adoring the newborn King. The stars and sweet-faced cherubs are fused onto a pieced background, and embroidery stitches are used to provide details.*

## You will need:

- Wonder-Under® transfer web
- fabrics for wall hanging top and binding (see **Table**, page 58)
- assorted fabrics for appliqués
- 29" x 37" piece of fabric for backing
- 7" x 24" piece of fabric for hanging sleeve
- 29" x 37" piece of polyester bonded batting
- fusible interfacing (optional)
- tear-away stabilizer
- yellow-gold and black embroidery floss
- gold cord
- metallic gold thread
- clear nylon thread
- pink fabric paint
- small paintbrush
- four 3½" lengths of mini gold star garland for halos
- two 9mm jingle bells
- quilting hoop or frame
- thread to match fabrics
- chalk pencil
- tracing paper
- pressing cloth

## PIECING WALL HANGING TOP

**1.** Wash, dry, and press fabrics.

**2.** Refer to **Table**, page 58, to cut fabrics for piecing wall hanging top.

**3.** (**Note:** For all sewing steps, match right sides and raw edges of fabrics, use a ¼" seam allowance, and press seam allowances to one side. Refer to **Assembly Diagram** and **Unit Key**, page 58, for piece placement.) Sew A, B, C, then D together to make **Unit 1**. Sew E, F, G, H, then I together to make **Unit 2**. Sew J, K, L, M, N, then O together to make **Unit 3**.

**4.** Sew **Unit 1**, **Unit 2**, then **Unit 3** together to complete center section of wall hanging.

**5.** Sew P to top of center section. Sew short edges of Q and R together; sew to bottom of center section. Sew short edges of S and T together; sew to left side of center section. Sew short edges of U and V together; sew to right side of center section.

**6.** Using patterns, pages 123 and 128, follow **Making Appliqués**, page 102, to make seven medium star appliqués; five (one in reverse) flying angel foot appliqués; four each of angel head and flying angel hand appliqués; two flying angel robe A appliqués; and one each of kneeling angel hand, kneeling angel foot, baby face, baby body, flying angel robe B, kneeling angel robe, large star, and manger appliqués.

**7.** Arrange appliqués on wall hanging top, overlapping as necessary; fuse in place.

**8.** Referring to patterns, use chalk pencil to draw sleeve lines on angel robes.

**9.** Using gold thread, follow **Machine Appliqué**, page 105, to stitch over raw edges of large star, manger star, and angel robe appliqués and to stitch along drawn sleeve lines. Using clear thread, follow **Machine Appliqué** to stitch over raw edges of remaining appliqués.

**10.** (**Note:** Refer to **Embroidery Stitches**, page 104, for Steps 10 - 15.) For each angel, use three strands of black floss to work a **French Knot** for each eye, one strand of black floss to work **Straight Stitches** for eyelashes, and two strands of black floss to work **Stem Stitch** for mouth. Use three strands of yellow-gold floss to work **Straight Stitches** for hair.

**11.** Use four strands of yellow-gold floss to work **Chain Stitch** for star chain and to sew one bell to end of chain and one to top of star on piece A.

**12.** Trace medium star pattern, page 128, onto tracing paper; cut out. Use chalk pencil to write "away in a manger" and draw around star pattern on piece O. Use twelve strands of yellow-gold floss to work **Running Stitch** for words.

**13.** For wings, use chalk pencil to draw desired wings on each angel. Use one strand of gold thread and work **Couching Stitch** to attach gold cord along drawn lines.

**14.** Use one strand of gold thread and work **Couching Stitch** to attach one length of star garland for each halo.

**15.** Use two strands of gold thread to work long **Running Stitches** for rays below large star.

**16.** Paint angel cheeks pink; allow to dry.

## QUILTING WALL HANGING

**1.** Place backing fabric wrong side up. Place batting on backing. Center wall hanging top, right side up, on batting. Pin layers together. Working from center outward, baste layers together from corner to corner. With basting lines 3" to 4" apart, baste from top to bottom and from side to side. Baste ¼" from each edge of wall hanging top.

**2.** Insert basted layers in hoop or frame, pulling fabrics taut. Working from center outward, use quilting thread and follow **Quilting**, page 105, to quilt wall hanging "in the ditch" (close to seamlines) along all seams; around each angel, large star, and entire manger and baby; and ¼" from rays below large star. Using gold thread, quilt ¼" inside edges of large star and along drawn lines for medium stars on piece O.

## FINISHING WALL HANGING

**1.** Trim batting and backing even with wall hanging top. Remove basting threads.

**2.** For bottom binding, sew bottom binding strips together at one short edge. Repeat for left binding and right binding.

**3.** Matching wrong sides, press each binding strip in half lengthwise; unfold. Press long raw edges to center.

| Table | | |
|---|---|---|
| **Piece** | **Size (width x length)** | **Fabric** |
| A | $9^1/2$" x $10^1/2$" | light blue print |
| B | $9^1/2$" x $1^1/2$" | gold print |
| C | $9^1/2$" x $2^1/2$" | blue check |
| D | $1^1/2$" x $13^1/2$" | gold print |
| E | $3^1/2$" x $3^1/2$" | blue check |
| F | $3^1/2$" x $3^1/2$" | blue print |
| G | $1^1/2$" x $6^1/2$" | dark gold print |
| H | $6^1/2$" x $6^1/2$" | brown print |
| I | $10^1/2$" x $7^1/2$" | light blue print |
| J | $3^1/2$" x $3^1/2$" | blue print |
| K | $3^1/2$" x $3^1/2$" | blue check |
| L | $3^1/2$" x $3^1/2$" | dark blue print |
| M | $1^1/2$" x $9^1/2$" | brown print |
| N | $16^1/2$" x $9^1/2$" | dark blue print |
| O | $20^1/2$" x $6^1/2$" | blue check |
| P | $20^1/2$" x $2^1/2$" | gold print |
| Q | $12^1/2$" x $2^1/2$" | dark gold print |
| R | $8^1/2$" x $2^1/2$" | brown print |
| S | $2^1/2$" x $23^1/2$" | gold print |
| T | $2^1/2$" x $9^1/2$" | dark gold print |
| U | $2^1/2$" x $9^1/2$" | gold print |
| V | $2^1/2$" x $23^1/2$" | brown print |
| Top binding | $24^1/2$" x $1^1/2$" | gold print |
| Bottom binding: | | |
| left strip | $14^1/2$" x $1^1/2$" | dark gold print |
| right strip | $10^1/2$" x $1^1/2$" | brown print |
| Left binding: | | |
| top strip | $1^1/2$" x $24^1/2$" | gold print |
| bottom strip | $1^1/2$" x $10^1/2$" | dark gold print |
| Right binding: | | |
| top strip | $1^1/2$" x $10^1/2$" | gold print |
| bottom strip | $1^1/2$" x $24^1/2$" | brown print |

**4.** To bind wall hanging, unfold one long edge of top binding strip. With right sides facing, match unfolded edge of binding strip to top edge of wall hanging; pin in place. Sew binding to wall hanging. Fold binding over to wall hanging backing; hand sew in place. Repeat for bottom edge of wall hanging.

**5.** Leaving $1^1/2$" of binding at each end, unfold one long edge of left binding strip. With right sides facing, match unfolded edge of binding strip to left edge of wall hanging; pin in place. Sew binding to wall hanging. Trim each end of binding $1/2$" longer than top and bottom edges; fold each end over to wall hanging backing. Fold binding strip over to wall hanging backing; hand sew in place. Repeat to add right binding strip to right side of wall hanging.

**6.** For hanging sleeve, press short edges of strip $1/4$" to wrong side; press $1/4$" to wrong side again. Stitch along first fold. Matching right sides and long edges, stitch $1/4$" from long edges to form a tube. Turn right side out and press. Center and pin sleeve to quilt back 1" below top edge. Hand sew both long edges to quilt back, taking care not to stitch through front of quilt.

**Assembly Diagram**

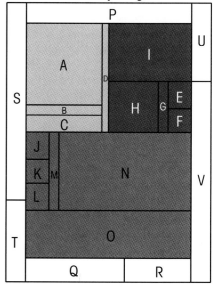

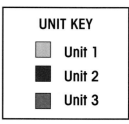

UNIT KEY
Unit 1
Unit 2
Unit 3

# HANDMADE HOLIDAY STOCKINGS

*A background of black wool provides a dramatic contrast for the vibrant appliqués on these handmade stockings. The quaint motifs are simply layered, fused together, and embellished with decorative stitching.*

**Note:** Supplies are for making one stocking.

**You will need:**
Heavy Duty Wonder-Under® transfer web
two 12" x 17" pieces of felt for stocking
12" x 17" piece of black felt for appliqué background
$1^5/8$" x $7^1/4$" strip of plaid fabric
scraps of felt for appliqués
embroidery floss to coordinate with appliqués
thread to match stocking felt
removable fabric marking pen
pinking shears
tracing paper
pressing cloth

## Flower Stocking

**1.** Matching grey lines and arrows, trace stocking top and stocking bottom patterns, page 125, onto tracing paper; cut out.

**2.** Place stocking fabric pieces wrong sides together. Center stocking pattern on fabric pieces and use removable pen to draw around pattern. Stitching directly on drawn lines and leaving top of stocking open, sew fabric pieces together. Use pinking shears to cut out stocking $1/4$" outside stitching line and drawn line at top of stocking.

**3.** Using stocking pattern, follow **Making Appliqués**, page 102, to make one background appliqué in reverse from black felt; do not remove paper backing.

**4.** Using patterns, page 125, follow **Making Appliqués** to make three each of outer flower, flower middle, flower center, and stem appliqués from felt scraps. Use pinking shears to trim edges of outer flowers. Arrange appliqués on background appliqué, overlapping as necessary; fuse in place.

**5.** Remove paper backing from background appliqué. Use three strands of floss and follow **Embroidery Stitches**, page 104, to work **Running Stitch** inside edge of outer flower

appliqués, **Blanket Stitch** along edges of remaining appliqués, and **Running Stitch** for tendrils.

**6.** Center background on stocking; fuse in place. Use three strands of floss to work **Blanket Stitch** around edges of background.

**7.** For hanger, fold $1^5/8$" x $7^1/4$" fabric strip in half lengthwise and use a $1/4$" seam allowance to sew long edges together. Use pinking shears to trim edges. Matching ends, fold strip in half. Place ends of hanger $1^1/2$" inside stocking at heel seam; make one large **Cross Stitch**, page 105, through front of stocking and ends of hanger to secure hanger to stocking.

## Bird Stocking

**1.** Follow Steps 1 - 3 of **Flower Stocking** instructions to make stocking.

**2.** Using patterns, page 125, follow **Making Appliqués** to make three each of bird and wing appliqués, thirteen leaf appliqués, and two heart appliqués from felt scraps. Arrange appliqués on background appliqué, overlapping as necessary; fuse in place.

**3.** Remove paper backing from background appliqué. Use three strands of floss and follow **Embroidery Stitches**, page 104, to work **Blanket Stitch** along edges of appliqués, a **French Knot** for each eye, and **Stem Stitches** for branches.

**4.** Follow Steps 6 and 7 of **Flower Stocking** instructions to complete stocking.

59

# PATCHWORK STOCKINGS

*Whether used as decorative accents or filled with surprises from Santa, these homespun stockings will please those who enjoy the look of quilted handcrafts. The holiday holders feature pieced cuffs with appliquéd heart and evergreen motifs and decorative prairie point edgings.*

**Note:** Supplies are for making one stocking.

**You will need:**
Wonder-Under® transfer web
two 12" x 20" pieces of cream print fabric for stocking
two 12" x 20" pieces of fabric for stocking lining
3" x 16" piece of cream plaid fabric for cuff
two 1¹/₂" x 16" pieces of red plaid fabric for cuff borders
5" x 16" piece of fabric for cuff lining
2" x 8" piece of fabric for hanger
six 4" squares of green check fabric for prairie points
two 5" squares of red plaid fabric for heel and toe appliqués
scraps of red or green fabric for cuff appliqués
tear-away stabilizer
clear nylon thread
tracing paper
pressing cloth

**Note:** Use a ¹/₄" seam allowance for all sewing steps, unless otherwise indicated.

**1.** Matching grey lines and arrows, trace stocking top and stocking bottom patterns, page 129, onto tracing paper. Draw a second line ¹/₄" outside first line; cut out along outer line.

**2.** Place stocking fabric pieces right sides together. Use pattern to cut out two stocking pieces. Repeat for lining pieces.

**3.** Using red plaid squares and patterns, page 129, follow **Making Appliqués**, page 102, to make one each of heel and toe appliqués. Fuse appliqués to stocking front piece. Use clear thread and follow **Machine Appliqué**, page 105, to stitch appliqués to stocking front piece.

**4.** Leaving top open for turning, sew stocking pieces together. Clip curves and turn right side out. Repeat for lining pieces; do not turn.

**5.** Place lining inside stocking, matching seams and raw edges; baste raw edges together.

**6.** Matching right sides, sew one cuff border to each long edge of cuff.

**7.** Using patterns, page 122, follow **Making Appliqués** to make three small heart appliqués or three small tree appliqués.

**8.** To make prairie points, fold each square in half diagonally with wrong sides together; fold in half again and press (**Fig. 1**).

**Fig. 1**

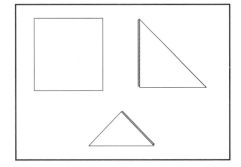

**9.** Arrange appliqués on cuff (**Fig. 2**) and fuse in place. Use clear thread and follow **Machine Appliqué** to stitch over raw edges of appliqués. Baste prairie points to bottom edge of cuff, overlapping as necessary (**Fig. 2**).

**Fig. 2**

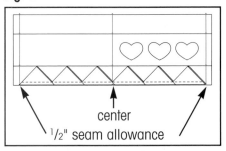

center
¹/₂" seam allowance

**10.** Matching right sides, sew cuff and cuff lining together along bottom edge, enclosing raw edges of prairie points in seam. Open and press. Matching right sides and short edges, fold cuff in half. Using a ¹/₂" seam allowance, sew short edges together to form a tube; turn right side out. Fold raw edge of lining to inside to meet raw edge of cuff; press.

**11.** For hanger, press long edges of 2" x 8" fabric piece ¹/₂" to wrong side. With wrong sides together, press in half lengthwise; stitch close to pressed edges. Fold hanger in half to form a loop. Matching raw edges of loop to raw edges of stocking at heel seam, pin hanger in place inside stocking.

**12.** Matching right side of cuff to stocking lining, raw edges, and cuff seam to heel seam, insert cuff in stocking; pin in place. Sew cuff to stocking through all layers. Turn cuff out over stocking.

# RUSTIC SNOWMAN

*Built with laughter and love, our rustic snowman radiates a childlike charm. His hand-sculpted shape stirs fond memories of the frosty days of our youth when we dressed our snow creations in hand-me-down hats and scarves.*

**You will need:**

two 9" x 16" pieces of muslin for snowman

2" x 10" piece of muslin for hat

two 3½" dia. and two 5" dia. circles of muslin for hat

3" x 4" piece of orange fabric for nose

1" x 15" piece of fabric for scarf

tan and red embroidery floss

polyester fiberfill

black acrylic paint

paintbrush

two ³⁄₈"w rocks for eyes

three ½"w rocks for buttons

two 5" long twigs for arms

1"h artificial bird

instant coffee

fabric marking pencil

seam ripper

thread to match fabrics

tracing paper

hot glue gun and glue sticks

**1.** Paint rocks black; allow to dry.

**2.** Dissolve two tablespoons instant coffee in two cups hot water; allow to cool. Soak muslin pieces in coffee several minutes; remove from coffee. Allow to dry and press.

**3.** Matching grey lines and arrows, trace snowman top and snowman bottom patterns, page 130, onto tracing paper; cut out.

**4.** Use pattern and follow **Sewing Shapes**, page 105, to make one snowman from 9" x 16" muslin pieces. Stuff snowman with fiberfill; sew final closure by hand.

**5.** To make indentations for eyes, nose, and buttons, thread a long needle with tan floss. Leaving a 2" tail of floss, insert needle from front to back of snowman; bring needle back up ⅛" away. Knot floss tightly to form a dimple; trim ends.

**6.** (**Note:** Use a ¼" seam allowance for all sewing steps unless otherwise indicated.) For nose, trace nose pattern, page 130, onto tracing paper; cut out. Use pattern to cut one nose

from orange fabric. Matching right sides and long edges, sew long edges together. Trim seam allowance to ⅛"; turn right side out. Stuff nose with fiberfill to within ½" of opening. Fold fabric over opening and tack in place.

**7.** Glue rocks and nose to snowman over knots at indentations. Use four strands of red floss to work **Running Stitch**, page 105, for mouth.

**8.** For arms, use seam ripper to open a ¼" long slit on each side of snowman. Apply glue to one end of each twig; insert twigs into slits.

**9.** Matching right sides and short edges, sew short edges of 2" x 10" muslin piece together to form a tube; press seam open. Fold raw edges ¼" to wrong side; press. Turn right side out.

**10.** Matching right sides and leaving an opening for turning, sew 3½" dia. circles together. Clip curves and turn

right side out; press. Sew final closure by hand. Repeat for 5" dia. circles.

**11.** For crown of hat, use two strands of red floss and **Straight Stitches** to stitch one edge of tube to edge of small circle (**Fig. 1**). Center crown on remaining circle and use **Straight Stitches** to stitch crown in place.

**Fig. 1**

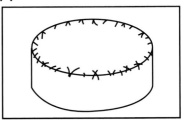

**12.** Glue hat on head; glue bird on one arm. Tie scarf around neck.

# SOFT POINSETTIA WREATH

*A lovely Yuletide accent, our soft poinsettia wreath is sure to garner compliments. The pretty fabric flowers and cheery bow are easily created by fusing together fabric and batting. For an impressive holiday display, the elements are wired onto an evergreen wreath.*

**You will need:**
Wonder Under® transfer web
20" dia. artificial wreath
red check, red print, and red plaid fabrics
assorted green print fabrics
fleece
black embroidery floss
fifteen 15mm wooden beads
floral wire
wire cutters
hot glue gun and glue sticks
pressing cloth

**1.** For poinsettia background, cut one 9" square each from web, fleece, and red fabric. Follow **Fusing Basics**, page 102, to fuse fabric to one side of fleece. Repeat to make a total of three poinsettia backgrounds.

**2.** Using patterns, page 131, follow **Making Appliqués**, page 102, to make three A appliqués from red check fabric, three B appliqués from red print fabric, and three C appliqués from red plaid fabric.

**3.** Arrange one set of appliqués on fleece side of one poinsettia background, overlapping as necessary; fuse in place. Cut out along outer edges only of appliqués. Repeat for remaining backgrounds.

**4.** Use wire cutters to cut three 6" lengths of wire; fold wire lengths in half. Insert ends of one wire length through front center of each poinsettia. Use six strands of black floss to sew five beads to center of each poinsettia, covering wire.

**5.** For leaf background, cut one 15" x 20" piece each from web, fleece, and green print fabric. Fuse fabric to one side of fleece.

**6.** Using patterns, page 131, follow **Making Appliqués** to make six leaf A appliqués from one green print and thirteen leaf B appliqués from a different green print.

**7.** Cut nineteen 6" lengths of floral wire.

**8.** Placing one wire length between fleece and appliqué, fuse leaf appliqués to background. Cut out along outer edge of each appliqué.

**9.** For bow streamer, cut two 4" x 36" pieces each from web and red plaid fabric and one 4" x 36" piece from fleece. Fuse one fabric piece to each side of fleece.

**10.** For back bow loop, cut two 4" x 27" pieces each from web and red print fabric and one 4" x 27" piece from fleece. Fuse one fabric piece to each side of fleece.

**11.** For top bow loop, cut two 4" x 19" pieces each from web and red plaid fabric and one 4" x 19" piece from fleece. Fuse one fabric piece to each side of fleece.

**12.** Overlapping ends 1", glue short edges of each loop piece together to form two circles.

**13.** With seams at back, place top loop over back loop. Place bow on streamer 17" from one end.

**14.** Cut an 18" length of wire. Wrap wire around bow and streamer. Twist wire ends together at back of bow to secure.

**15.** For knot, cut a 4" x 7" piece of red plaid fabric. Wrap fabric around center of loops, covering wire. Glue ends to back of streamer.

**16.** Cut V-shaped notches in each streamer end.

**17.** Arrange bow, poinsettias, and leaves on wreath. Use wire on back of each piece to secure to wreath.

# COUNTRY STOCKINGS

*Let country charm mark your decorating mood, starting with these cozy, old-fashioned stockings! Crafted for down-home appeal, the long stockings feature simple embroidered names on the cuffs. The sock stockings are dressed up with fabric heels and toes, stars, and buttons.*

## Sock Stocking

**Note:** Supplies are for making one stocking.

**You will need:**
Wonder-Under® transfer web
one men's calf-length white sock with heel and 1¹/₂"w ribbing
assorted fabrics for heel, toe, and star appliqués
black embroidery floss
buttons
instant coffee
6" length of ¹/₄"w braided jute twine for hanger
tracing paper
pressing cloth

**1.** Dissolve two tablespoons instant coffee in two cups hot water; allow to cool. Soak sock in coffee several minutes; remove from coffee. Allow to dry.

**2.** Trace sock stocking pattern, page 133, onto tracing paper; cut out.

**3.** Aligning heel seams, press sock flat. Arrange pattern on sock, matching front edge of sock to pattern as closely as possible and aligning pattern heel even with sock heel. Pin pattern in place. Leaving top of sock uncut, cut through both layers of sock along bottom and heel side of pattern.

**Fig. 1**

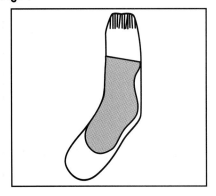

**4.** Using patterns, page 133, follow **Making Appliqués**, page 102, to make one each of heel and toe appliqués and two (one in reverse) star appliqués.

**5.** Arrange toe and heel appliqués on front of sock, matching outer edges; fuse in place. Use six strands of black floss to work **Blanket Stitch**, page 104, along inner edges of heel and toe and to sew buttons to front of sock.

**6.** Turn sock wrong side out. Tapering stitching at beginning and end of seam to meet uncut edges of sock, use a ¹/₄" seam allowance to sew cut edges of sock together. Turn sock right side out and press.

**7.** Fuse star appliqués together. Center one button on star and sew button and star to stocking.

**8.** For hanger, fold jute in half to form a loop. Place ends of hanger inside stocking at heel seam; tack in place.

## Long Stocking

**Note:** Supplies are for making one stocking.

**You will need:**
two 12" x 23" pieces of fabric for stocking
two 12" x 23" pieces of fabric for lining
10" x 11" piece of fabric for cuff
black embroidery floss
buttons
6" length of ¹/₄"w braided jute twine for hanger
removable fabric marking pen
thread to match fabrics
tracing paper

**1.** Matching grey lines and arrows, trace long stocking top and long stocking bottom patterns, page 132, onto tracing paper; cut out.

**2.** Using stocking pattern and leaving top edge open, follow **Sewing Shapes**, page 105, to make stocking from stocking fabric pieces. Repeat for lining pieces; do not turn.

**3.** With wrong sides together, insert lining into stocking. Baste top edges of lining and stocking together.

**4.** (**Note:** Use a ¹/₂" seam allowance for remaining steps.) For cuff, match right sides and short edges of cuff fabric piece; sew short edges together to form a tube. Press seam open; turn cuff right side out. Matching wrong sides and raw edges, fold cuff in half.

**5.** Matching right side of cuff to stocking lining, raw edges, and cuff seam to heel seam, insert cuff in stocking; pin in place. Sew cuff to stocking through all layers. Turn cuff out over stocking.

**6.** Use removable pen to write name on cuff. Use six strands of black floss and **Running Stitch**, page 105, to stitch name on cuff and to sew buttons along bottom edge of cuff.

**7.** For hanger, fold jute in half to form a loop. Place ends of hanger inside stocking at heel seam; tack in place.

# gifts for all

**T**his season, create presents as individual as the people on your gift list! It's fun — and almost effortless — with the help of Pellon® Wonder-Under® transfer web and our quick crafting techniques. In this cheery collection, you'll find delightful accents to convey season's greetings, festive frames and photo albums to showcase Christmas memories, and lots of clever containers for delivering goodies. Easy to make and easy to love, these handcrafted gifts will be wonderful reminders of your warm holiday wishes.

# "RECYCLED" GIFT CANS

*Feeling boxed in by traditional gift wraps? Then craft one or all of these "recycled" gift cans to deliver some of your seasonal surprises! The fabric-lined holders are made from clean, dry food cans, which are primed, spray painted, and decorated with fabric-covered poster board cutouts.*

## Reindeer Can

**You will need:**
Wonder-Under® transfer web
$4^1/_2$"h x $6^1/_8$" dia. clean, dry can
white spray primer
green spray paint
matte clear acrylic spray sealer
fabric for appliqué
16" square of fabric for liner
$3/_8$" x 10" strip of fabric for bow
poster board
one small black button
one 8mm red bead
twigs
hot glue gun and glue sticks
pressing cloth

**1.** Allowing to dry between coats, spray can with primer, paint, and then sealer.

**2.** Using reindeer pattern, page 134, follow **Making Appliqués**, page 102, to make one reindeer appliqué.

**3.** Fuse appliqué to poster board; cut out.

**4.** Glue button to reindeer for eye, bead to reindeer for nose, and twigs to back of reindeer's head for antlers.

**5.** Tie fabric strip into a bow. Glue bow to reindeer's neck. Glue reindeer to can.

**6.** Fringe edges of each side of fabric square for liner. Place liner in can.

## Shooting Stars Can

**You will need:**
Wonder-Under® transfer web
$6^5/_8$"h x $6^1/_8$" dia. clean, dry can
white spray primer
burgundy spray paint
matte clear acrylic spray sealer
assorted fabric scraps for appliqués
22" square of fabric for liner
poster board
black permanent pen
twigs
26" length of jute twine
hot glue gun and glue sticks
pressing cloth

**1.** Allowing to dry between coats, spray can with primer, paint, and then sealer.

**2.** Using patterns, pages 134 and 135, follow **Making Appliqués**, page 102, to make three medium star appliqués and one each of large star and label appliqués.

**3.** Arrange appliqués on poster board, overlapping as necessary; fuse in place. Cutting around outer edges of design, cut out appliqués.

**4.** Use pen to write "Peace," "Love," or "Joy" on medium stars, greeting on label, and draw "stitches" around label.

**5.** Glue each medium star to end of one twig. Glue opposite ends of each twig to back of large star. Glue stars to can.

**6.** Fringe edges of each side of fabric square for liner. Place liner in can. Tie jute into a bow around top of liner.

## Evergreen Can

**You will need:**
Wonder-Under® transfer web
$4^5/_8$"h x 4" dia. clean, dry can
white spray primer
cream spray paint
matte clear acrylic spray sealer
assorted fabric scraps for appliqués
$15^1/_2$" square of fabric for liner
poster board
four 8mm red beads
hot glue gun and glue sticks
pressing cloth

**1.** Allowing to dry between coats, spray can with primer, paint, and then sealer.

**2.** Using patterns, page 135, follow **Making Appliqués**, page 102, to make one each of small star, small tree, and tree trunk appliqués.

**3.** Arrange appliqués on poster board, overlapping as necessary; fuse in place. Cutting around outer edges of design, cut out appliqués.

**4.** Glue beads to tree. Glue tree to can.

**5.** Fringe edges of each side of fabric square for liner. Place liner in can.

## Snowman Can

**You will need:**
Wonder-Under® transfer web
$4^3/_8$"h x $2^7/_8$" dia. clean, dry can
white spray primer
burgundy spray paint
matte clear acrylic spray sealer
assorted fabric scraps for appliqués
15" square of fabric for liner
poster board
$1/_2$" dia. white pom-pom
black permanent pen
hot glue gun and glue sticks
pressing cloth

**1.** Allowing to dry between coats, spray can with primer, paint, and then sealer.

**2.** Using patterns, pages 134 and 135, follow **Making Appliqués**, page 102, to make one each of snowman, snowman hat, label, hand A, hand B, and snowman nose appliqués.

**3.** Arrange appliqués on poster board, overlapping as necessary; fuse in place. Cutting around outer edges of design, cut out appliqués.

**4.** Use pen to add eyes and mouth to snowman, write greeting on label, and draw "stitches" around label. Glue pom-pom to tip of hat. Glue snowman to can.

**5.** Fringe edges of each side of fabric square for liner. Place liner in can.

## Santa Can

**You will need:**
Wonder-Under® transfer web
$6^5/_8$"h x $6^1/_8$" dia. clean, dry can
white spray primer
cream spray paint
matte clear acrylic spray sealer
assorted fabric scraps for appliqués
fusible interfacing (optional)
22" square of fabric for liner
poster board
two black buttons
black permanent pen
hot glue gun and glue sticks
pressing cloth

**1.** Allowing to dry between coats, spray can with primer, paint, and then sealer.

**2.** Using patterns, page 134, follow **Making Appliqués**, page 102, to make one each of Santa face, Santa hat, mustache, hat trim/beard, and Santa nose appliqués.

**3.** Arrange appliqués on poster board, overlapping as necessary; fuse in place. Cutting around outer edges of design, cut out appliqués.

**4.** Glue buttons to face for eyes. Use pen to draw mouth. Glue Santa to can.

**5.** Fringe edges of each side of fabric square for liner. Place liner in can.

# CHRISTMAS TREE COASTERS

*This cheery set will make the holidays more pleasant for a friend who enjoys entertaining. The handy Christmas tree-shaped coasters are easy to make by fusing fleece between layers of fabric. Buttons and bows top off the sweet accents.*

**Note:** Supplies are for making one coaster.

**You will need:**
Wonder-Under® transfer web
two 7" squares of green print fabric
7" square of craft fleece
$5/8$" x 5" torn strip of fabric for bow
$1/2$" dia. button
pinking shears
removable fabric marking pen
tracing paper
pressing cloth

**1.** Follow **Fusing Basics**, page 102, to fuse one fabric square to each side of fleece.

**2.** Trace large tree pattern, page 135, onto tracing paper; cut out. Use removable pen to trace around pattern on one side of square. Use pinking shears to cut out tree.

**3.** Shape fabric strip into a bow and wrap thread around center to secure. Sew button to center of bow; sew bow to top of tree.

# CORDIAL SNOWMAN

*Our simple snowman bottle bag lets you make a special delivery of holiday spirits! The coffee-dyed bag is easy to fuse together and is accented with buttons, a rag-strip scarf, and a quaint top hat.*

**You will need:**
Wonder-Under® fusible tape
bottle
muslin
2" x 16" torn strip of fabric for scarf
1/2" x 7" strip of fabric for hat trim
orange acrylic paint
small paintbrush
3" dia. black felt top hat
1/4" x 3" stick for nose
1"h artificial bird
red permanent pen
two 1/2" dia. shank buttons for eyes
three 3/4" dia. buttons for front of
    snowman
instant coffee
craft knife
tissue paper
two rubber bands
hot glue gun and glue sticks
pressing cloth

**1.** Measure around bottle; add 2". Measure bottle from top to center of bottom (**Fig. 1**); add 7". Cut a piece of muslin the determined measurements.

**Fig. 1**

**2.** Dissolve one tablespoon instant coffee in one cup hot water; allow to cool. Soak muslin in coffee several minutes. Remove from coffee and allow to dry; press.

**3.** To make bag, follow **Fusing Basics**, page 102, to press fusible tape along one short, then one long edge on right side of muslin; remove paper backing from long edge. Matching right sides and long edges, fold muslin in half; fuse in place. Remove paper backing from short edge. Fold tube with seam at center back (**Fig. 2**); fuse in place. Turn bag right side out.

**Fig. 2**

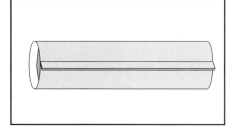

**4.** Place bottle in bag. For head, wrap one rubber band around bag 3" below top of bottle. Stuff tissue paper into bag around top of bottle, forming a round shape. Wrap remaining rubber band around fabric bag just above top of bottle.

**5.** Fold bottom corners of bag under bottle; glue to secure.

**6.** For scarf, tie torn fabric strip around snowman's neck.

**7.** For nose, use craft knife to shape one end of stick to a point; cut 1" from pointed end of stick. Paint nose orange; allow to dry. Glue nose to head. Glue 1/2" dia. buttons to head for eyes. Use pen to draw mouth.

**8.** Glue 3/4" dia. buttons to front of snowman.

**9.** Glue remaining fabric strip around hat and bird to brim of hat. Place hat on head.

# CROCHETED TOTE

*Here's a fun gift that can be enjoyed all through the season! Our roomy Christmas tote is fast to finish because it's crocheted with fabric strips and a jumbo hook. Fill the holder with surprises for two gifts in one.*

**Rnd 2:** Ch 1, sc in same st, 3 sc in next sc, sc in next 9 sc, 3 sc in next sc, sc in each sc around; join with slip st to first sc: 24 sc.

**Rnd 3:** Ch 1, 2 sc in same st, (sc in next sc, 2 sc in next sc) twice, sc in next 7 sc, 2 sc in next sc, (sc in next sc, 2 sc in next sc) twice, sc in each sc around; join with slip st to Back Loop Only of first sc (**Fig. 2**): 30 sc.

**Fig. 2**

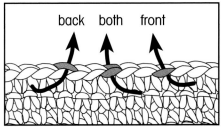

**Rnd 4:** Ch 1, sc in Back Loop Only of each sc around; join with slip st to both loops of first sc.

**Rnds 5 - 13:** Ch 1, sc in both loops of each sc around; join with slip st to first sc changing to CC at end of Rnd 13 (**Fig. 3**).

**Fig. 3**

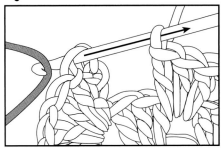

**Rnd 14:** Ch 1, sc in each sc around; join with slip st to first sc.

**Rnd 15:** Ch 1, sc in first 10 sc, ch 20 (handle), skip next 5 sc, sc in next 10 sc, ch 20 (handle), skip last 5 sc; join with slip st to first sc: 20 sc.

**Edging:** Slip st in each sc and in each ch around; join with slip st to first slip st, finish off.

**You will need:**
5 yds of 44/45"w 100% cotton fabric for main color (MC)
1¹/₈ yds of 44/45"w 100% cotton fabric for contrasting color (CC)
crochet hook, size Q or size needed for gauge

**Note:** Follow **Preparing Fabric Strips**, page 104, to tear fabric into 2"w strips. Refer to **Crochet**, page 103, before beginning project.

**Gauge:** 6 sc = 5¹/₂"
5 rows = 4"
Rnds 1 - 3 = 5" x 11¹/₂"

With MC, ch 10 **loosely**.

**Rnd 1** (Right side): 3 Sc in second ch from hook, sc in next 7 chs, 3 sc in last ch; working in free loops of beginning ch (**Fig. 1**), sc in next 7 chs; join with slip st to first sc: 20 sc.

**Fig. 1**

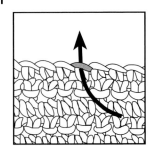

# CHEERY KITCHEN TOWELS

*These cute towels will bring cheer to the Christmas kitchen! Mr. and Mrs. Snowman are cut
from felt and fabric, fused onto purchased towels, and machine appliquéd with clear nylon thread.
With these lasting gifts, your thoughtfulness will be remembered for many Yuletides to come.*

**You will need:**
Heavy Duty Wonder-Under®
   transfer web
two purchased kitchen towels
acrylic felt for face appliqués
assorted fabrics for appliqués
black and grey embroidery floss
tear-away stabilizer
clear nylon thread
assorted buttons
tracing paper
pressing cloth

**1.** Wash, dry, and press towels and fabrics.

**2.** Using patterns, page 136, follow **Making Appliqués**, page 102, to make four eye appliqués; two (one in reverse) nose appliqués; two snowman head appliqués; and one each of snowman hat, snow lady hat, holly, flower, pipe, snowman tie, and snow lady tie appliqués.

**3.** Arrange appliqués on towels, overlapping as necessary; fuse in place.

**4.** Using clear thread, follow **Machine Appliqué**, page 105, to stitch over raw edges of appliqués.

**5.** Use four strands of black floss to work **Running Stitch**, page 105, for mouths, and **Straight Stitch**, page 105, for snow lady eyelashes. Use three strands of grey floss to work **Running Stitch** for pipe smoke.

**6.** Sew one button to center of flower and each tie. Sew buttons to holly for berries.

# CHRISTMAS WAGON

*For a touch of Christmas whimsy, share this miniature wagon with someone who's young at heart!*
*Perfect for displaying an arrangement of holiday gifts or goodies, the wooden piece is simply painted*
*and decorated with ribbon and fused-on cutouts of fabric print ornaments and peppermint candies.*

**You will need:**
Heavy Duty Wonder-Under®
    transfer web
unfinished wooden wagon (ours
    measures 11"w x 16¹/₂"l x 6"h)
fabric with large Christmas motifs
¹/₈"w green satin ribbon
one 24" length each of ¹/₈"w red
    satin ribbon, ¹/₄"w green satin
    ribbon, and ¹/₄"w green
    grosgrain ribbon
red, green, and antique white
    acrylic paint
oil base stain
foam brushes
clean, soft cloth
fine-grit sand paper
tack cloth
craft glue
pressing cloth

**1.** Disassemble wagon and sand each piece; wipe with tack cloth.

**2.** Using a clean foam brush for each paint color, paint outside, inside, and tongue of wagon red; handle and outside of wheels antique white; and axle ends, wheel rims, and top edge of wagon green. Allow to dry. Reassemble wagon.

**3.** Use a pencil and ruler to lightly draw a line around wagon ¹/₂" from top edge.

**4.** Aligning bottom edge of ¹/₈"w green ribbon with pencil line, glue ribbon to wagon; allow to dry.

**5.** Follow **Fusing Basics**, page 102, to press web to wrong side of fabric. Cut out desired motifs for appliqués.

**6.** Arrange appliqués on wagon, overlapping as desired; fuse in place.

**7.** Follow manufacturer's instructions to apply stain to entire wagon. Remove excess stain with soft cloth until desired effect is achieved; allow to dry. Repeat if darker color is desired.

**8.** Tie 24" ribbon lengths into a bow around handle.

# TEATIME COZIES

*Lend old-fashioned flair to your gift-giving with this nostalgic tea cozy and coaster ensemble. Sewn from Christmas-green fabric and embellished with an assortment of ribbons, lace, buttons, and charms, this lovely set will remind a friend to take time to relax during the busy season.*

## Teapot Cozy

**You will need:**
Heavy Duty Wonder-Under® transfer web
two 15" x 20" pieces of decorative fabric
two 15" x 20" pieces of fabric for lining
two 15" x 20" pieces of craft fleece fabric for binding
items to decorate cozy (we used ribbons, lace, doilies, buttons, and charms)
aluminum foil
tracing paper
pressing cloth

**1.** Follow **Tracing Patterns**, page 105, to trace tea cozy pattern, page 137, onto tracing paper. Use pattern to cut two each from decorative fabric, fleece, and lining fabric.

**2.** Follow **Fusing Basics**, page 102, to fuse one lining piece to one side of fleece and one decorative fabric piece to opposite side of fleece to make cozy front. Repeat with remaining pieces to make cozy back.

**3.** Follow **Foil Method**, page 102, to press web to wrong side of desired ribbons, lace, and doilies. Arrange items on cozy front as desired; fuse in place. Trim ends even with edges of cozy front.

**4.** With lining sides facing, place cozy front and back together; baste all layers together 1/4" from raw edge.

**5.** Follow **Binding**, page 102, to add 2 1/2"w sewn binding around opening and top edge of cozy.

**6.** Use decorative items to decorate cozy front as desired.

## Coaster

**You will need:**
two 4 1/2" squares of Heavy Duty Wonder-Under® transfer web
two 4 1/2" squares of decorative fabric
4 1/2" square of craft fleece fabric for binding
items to decorate coaster (we used ribbons, lace, buttons, and charms)
aluminum foil
pressing cloth

**1.** Follow **Fusing Basics**, page 102, to fuse one decorative fabric square to each side of fleece square.

**2.** Follow **Foil Method**, page 102, to press web to wrong side of desired ribbons and lace. Arrange items on top side of coaster as desired; fuse in place. Trim ends even with edges of fabric.

**3.** Follow **Binding**, page 102, to add 2 1/2"w sewn binding to raw edges of coaster.

**4.** Use decorative items to decorate coaster top as desired.

# FESTIVE FRAMES

*Surprise a proud grandparent or a dear friend with a snapshot tucked in one of these elegant frames! An endearing way to show off photographs of loved ones, the holders are easily crafted by embellishing frames and mats with festive fabrics and shiny trims.*

## Padded Christmas Frame

**You will need:**
- 5" x 7" mat with oval opening
- 5" x 7" piece of cardboard for frame back
- 2" x 6" piece of cardboard for frame stand
- 7" x 9" piece of fabric to cover frame front
- 7" x 15¹/₂" piece of fabric to cover frame back
- 4" x 14" piece of fabric to cover frame stand
- low-loft polyester batting
- 1¹/₄ yds of ¹/₄" dia. gold twisted cord
- fabric marking pencil
- craft glue
- hot glue gun and glue sticks

**1.** (**Note:** Use hot glue for all gluing unless otherwise indicated.) Center mat on wrong side of fabric. Use pencil to draw around mat opening. Cutting 1" from drawn line, cut out oval (**Fig. 1**); clip fabric to ¹/₄" from drawn line.

**Fig. 1**

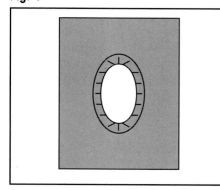

**2.** Using mat as a pattern, cut a piece of batting. Glue batting to mat. Center mat, batting side down, on wrong side of fabric. Fold fabric edges at opening of mat to back; glue in place. Fold corners of fabric diagonally over corners of mat (**Fig. 2**); glue in place. Fold remaining fabric edges to back of mat; glue in place.

**Fig. 2**

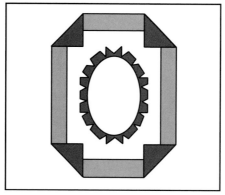

**3.** (**Note:** To prevent ends of cord from fraying after cutting, apply craft glue ¹/₂" around area to be cut, allow to dry, and then cut.) Hot glue a length of cord along edge of frame front, trimming to fit. Beginning and ending at bottom right of opening, repeat for frame front opening. Cut a 12" length of cord and tie into a bow; trim and fray ends. Glue bow to frame front, covering ends of cord around opening.

**4.** Place cardboard for frame back on wrong side of fabric for frame back (**Fig. 3**). Fold side edges of fabric over side edges of frame back; glue in place. Fold bottom edge of fabric over frame back; glue in place. Fold top edge of fabric 1" to wrong side; glue in place. Fold top half of fabric over frame back; glue along edges to secure.

**Fig. 3**

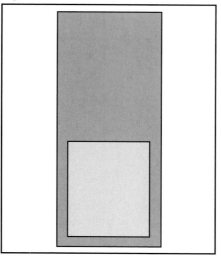

**5.** Glue side and bottom edges of frame back to back of frame front, leaving an opening at top for inserting photo.

**6.** Using cardboard and fabric for frame stand, repeat Step 4 to cover frame stand. Fold top 1¹/₂" of frame stand to right side. Centering wrong side of frame stand on back of frame and matching bottom of frame stand with bottom of frame, glue area of frame stand above fold to back of frame.

## Christmas Box Frame

**You will need:**
- 8" x 10" x 1¹/₂" plastic box frame with cardboard insert
- desired photo (5" x 7" or smaller)
- fabric to cover insert
- ¹/₂"w gimp trim
- ¹/₄"w flat trim
- ⁷/₈"w satin ribbon
- spray adhesive
- fabric marking pencil
- hot glue gun and glue sticks

**1.** To cover insert, remove cardboard insert from frame. Use fabric pencil to draw around insert on wrong side of fabric. Cut out fabric 1¹/₂" outside drawn lines. Make a diagonal clip at each corner of fabric from corner to ¹/₈" from drawn lines (**Fig. 1**).

**Fig. 1**

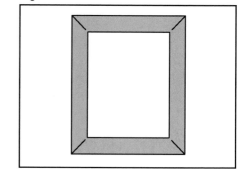

**2.** Apply spray adhesive to front and sides of insert. Center insert, front side down, on wrong side of fabric. Referring to **Fig. 2**, press long edges of fabric onto sides of insert; press clipped ends around corners of insert onto short sides. At each short edge of fabric, fold clipped ends of short edges to wrong side (**Fig. 2**). Press short edges of fabric onto sides of insert; glue corners in place.

**Fig. 2**

**3.** Making sure hanger on back of insert is at top, use spray adhesive to glue photo to center front of insert. Place insert in frame.

**4.** Beginning at center top of photo, glue gimp trim to frame, covering edges of photo. Glue flat trim over gimp trim.

**5.** Tie ribbon into a bow. Glue bow over ends of trims. Use small dots of glue to tack streamers in place.

# FIRESIDE PICNIC BASKET

*Make a couple's first Christmas together especially romantic with this charming picnic basket. Perfect for fireside dining, the wicker basket features a padded fabric-covered lid that has a handy mitten pocket for holding cutlery and napkins.*

**You will need:**
Wonder-Under® transfer web
Wonder-Under® fusible tape
$18^1/2$"l x 11"w x $5^1/2$"h oval basket with handle
$1^1/2$ yds of 44/45"w plaid flannel fabrics for lid lining, basket lining, padded bottom, and welting
$1/2$ yd of 44/45"w plaid flannel fabrics for lid and hinge
two 8" squares of plaid flannel fabric for mitten
19" square of plaid flannel fabric for napkin
two 28" lengths of 3"w grosgrain ribbon
polyester bonded batting
craft fleece (one 8" square and one 1" x 5" piece)
$1^5/8$ yds of $1/2$" dia. cord for welting
thread to match napkin fabric
two pieces of cardboard (measuring slightly larger than top of basket)
poster board (same size as cardboard)
tracing paper
two knives
two forks
hot glue gun and glue sticks
pressing cloth

## MAKING THE LINING

**1.** For basket lining, measure height of basket; add $2^1/2$". Measure around basket at widest part; add 2". Cut a piece of fabric the determined measurements.

**2.** Press one long edge and one short edge $1/2$" to wrong side.

**3.** Matching inside of basket to wrong side of fabric and beginning at short raw edge, glue long pressed edge along inner top edge of basket. Overlap short edges and glue in place.

**4.** For padded bottom, place basket on one piece of cardboard and draw around bottom of basket. Cut out cardboard $1/2$" inside drawn line.

Using cardboard as a pattern, cut one each of batting and web.

**5.** Leaving at least $1^1/2$" of fabric around edge of web, follow **Fusing Basics**, page 102, to press web to wrong side of lid fabric piece. Cut out fabric $1^1/2$" outside edge of web. Make clips in edge of fabric to $1/8$" from edge of web. Remove paper backing and fuse to batting.

**6.** Center cardboard on batting side of fabric piece. Alternating sides and pulling fabric taut, glue clipped edges of fabric to wrong side of cardboard.

**7.** Straighten folds in fabric and glue padded bottom to inside of basket over lining.

## MAKING PADDED LID

**1.** For each lid piece, align one straight edge of cardboard with edge of work surface. Turn basket upside down on cardboard with basket handles against edge of cardboard. Draw around basket on cardboard (**Fig. 1**). Cut out cardboard pieces.

**Fig. 1**

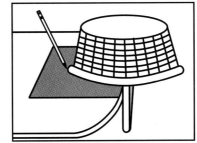

**2.** Trace cardboard pieces onto poster board. Cut out poster board $1/2$" inside drawn lines.

**3.** Using cardboard pieces as patterns, cut one piece each from batting and web for each cardboard piece.

**4.** Follow Steps 5 and 6 of **Making the Lining** to cover each lid piece.

**5.** For welting on each lid piece, measure curved edge of one padded lid to determine length of cord. Cut a piece of cord the determined measurement. Cut a $3^1/2$"w bias strip of fabric 2" longer than cord.

**6.** Press fusible tape along wrong side of one long edge of fabric strip. Center cord on wrong side of strip. Matching long edges, fuse edges together.

**7.** Matching welting to curved edge of lid, glue raw edge of welting to wrong side of lid.

**8.** Position padded lid pieces on basket. Measure width of opening between lid pieces; measure length of opening between handle. Cut one piece of web the determined measurement. Add 1" to width and length. Cut two fabric strips the determined measurement. Press short edges of each fabric strip $1/2$" to wrong side.

**9.** Center and press web to wrong side of one fabric strip. Fold ribbon lengths in half. Matching wrong sides and placing $1/2$" of fold of one ribbon length at center of each short edge between strips, fuse strips together to make hinge.

**10.** To attach hinge, place padded lid pieces wrong side up on basket. Center hinge between lid pieces. Glue each long edge to secure. Remove lid from basket.

**11.** Omitting batting and fusing fabric to poster board, follow Steps 5 and 6 of **Making the Lining** to cover poster board pieces to make lid linings.

**12.** With wrong sides together, glue a lining piece to wrong side of each lid piece. Place lid on basket and tie ribbons into bows around handle.

## MAKING THE MITTEN AND NAPKIN

**1.** Trace mitten pattern, page 138, onto tracing paper; cut out. Draw around pattern on 8" square of craft fleece; do not cut out.

**2.** Matching right sides and raw edges, place mitten fabric squares together. Place craft fleece square on fabric squares with drawn pattern facing up; pin layers together. Leaving straight edge open for turning, machine stitch directly on drawn lines through all layers; remove pins. Leaving a $1/4$" seam allowance, cut out mitten; clip curves and turn right side out. Using a $1/4$" seam allowance, sew across straight edge through all layers.

**3.** For mitten trim, glue 1" x 5" piece of craft fleece to one side of mitten along straight edge, wrapping short edges to back of mitten.

**4.** Leaving straight edge of mitten open, glue edges of mitten to padded lid.

**5.** Fold and press raw edges of napkin fabric $1/4$" to wrong side; fold and press $1/4$" to wrong side again. Using an $1/8$" seam allowance, machine stitch along napkin edges.

**6.** Insert napkin, knives, and forks into mitten.

# HOLIDAY BATH BASKET

*Delight a friend with our ruffled holiday bath basket filled with lots of goodies! Assorted fabrics are layered to create the padded holder, and the coordinating no-sew sachet bags are filled with potpourri. For a lovely finish, glue festive fabric motifs to miniature soaps and include a purchased bath mitt.*

## Basket

**You will need:**
Wonder-Under® fusible tape
round wicker basket
assorted fabrics to cover basket
embroidery floss to match fabric
polyester fiberfill
26" length of 1½"w grosgrain
    ribbon
fabric marking pencil
2½" dia. jingle bell
natural excelsior
string
thumbtack
hot glue gun and glue sticks
pressing cloth

**1.** For fabric to cover basket, measure basket from one side of rim to opposite side of rim (**Fig. 1**); add 9". Cut two squares of fabric the determined measurement.

**Fig. 1**

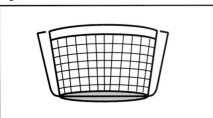

**2.** Matching right sides, fold one fabric square in half from top to bottom and again from left to right. Tie one end of string to fabric marking pencil. Measure ½ the measurement determined in Step 1 from pencil; insert thumbtack through string at this point. Insert thumbtack through fabric as shown in **Fig. 2** and mark cutting line. Cutting through all layers, cut out circle. Repeat to cut a second circle from remaining fabric square.

**Fig. 2**

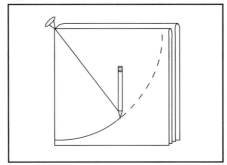

**3.** Follow **Fusing Basics**, page 102, to press fusible tape along edge of one fabric circle on right side of fabric. Leaving a 6" length of paper backing on tape for turning, match right sides of fabric circles and fuse edges together. Make clips in edge of fabric to ⅛" from inner edge of tape. Turn circles right side out. Remove remaining paper backing and fuse final closure.

**4.** To make inner ruffles, measure around top of basket; multiply by 2. Cut one strip of fabric 7"w by the determined measurement from two different fabrics.

**5.** For each ruffle, press fusible tape along right side of one short end of strip. Matching right sides and short ends, fuse ends together to form a circle. Press fusible tape along wrong side of one long edge of circle. Matching wrong sides and raw edges, fuse long edges together. Use embroidery floss to baste 2" from finished edge on each ruffle.

**6.** Stack ruffles on inside of fabric circle. Pull ends of floss to gather until finished edge of ruffle matches outer edge of fabric circle; pin in place. Use six strands of embroidery floss to hand baste layers together 2" from edge.

**7.** Place basket in center of fabric circle. Pull ends of floss to begin gathering fabric around basket. Fill space between basket and fabric with desired amount of fiberfill. Pull ends of floss to tighten fabric around top of basket; knot ends together. Adjust gathers as necessary.

**8.** Glue inner ruffle to top edge of basket to secure.

**9.** Thread bell to center of ribbon length. Tie ribbon into a bow; tack bow to edge of basket between ruffles.

**10.** Fill basket with excelsior, sachet bags, and soaps.

## Sachet Bags

**Note:** Supplies are for making one potpourri bag.

**You will need:**
Wonder-Under® fusible tape
7" x 9" piece of fabric
17½" length of ¾"w grosgrain
    ribbon
potpourri
pinking shears

**1.** Follow **Fusing Basics**, page 102, to press fusible tape along one long edge and one short edge on right side of fabric piece.

**2.** Matching right sides and short edges, fold fabric in half; fuse edges together. Turn bag right side out.

**3.** Use pinking shears to trim top edge of bag.

**4.** Fill bag with potpourri to 2" from top.

**5.** Tie ribbon into a bow around top of bag.

## Soaps

**Note:** Soaps are for decorative purposes only.

**You will need:**
miniature soaps
motif(s) cut from fabric
foam brush
craft glue

**1.** Mix one part glue with one part water.

**2.** Use glue mixture and foam brush to paint back of desired motif. Arrange motif on soap and smooth in place; allow to dry.

**3.** Use foam brush to lightly paint over motif with glue mixture; allow to dry.

# HOMEY SANTA BASKET

*Gift-giving is more fun than ever when treats are delivered in our homey Santa basket! Created by topping a basket with a drawstring bag, our jolly old gentleman is "dressed" in a color-block shirt made from Christmasy fabrics.*

**You will need:**
Wonder-Under® fusible tape
6¹/₂" dia. x 3¹/₂"h basket with
   handle
two 6" squares of muslin for head
four 4" x 9" pieces of muslin for
   arms
two 7" x 9" pieces of fabric for hat
7" x 22" piece of fabric for shirt
1⁵/₈" x 7" strip of fabric for placket
two 7" x 8" pieces of fabric for
   sleeves
1⁵/₈" x 23" strip of fabric for belt
thread to match fabrics
1 yd of ¹/₄"w ribbon
six ³/₈" dia. buttons
two ³/₁₆" dia. black shank buttons
   for eyes
7" length of 32-gauge spool wire
   for glasses
braided doll hair
powder blush
tracing paper
polyester fiberfill
hot glue gun and glue sticks
pressing cloth

**1.** Trace hat, Santa head, and arm patterns, page 137, onto tracing paper; cut out. Using patterns, follow **Sewing Shapes**, page 105, to make one each of head and hat and two arms. Follow **Fusing Basics**, page 102, to press fusible tape along wrong side of bottom edge of hat. Fold edge ¹/₂" to wrong side; fuse in place. Stuff head and arms with fiberfill; sew final closures by hand.

**2.** Sew buttons to center of face for eyes.

**3.** For cheeks, use fingertip to apply blush under eyes.

**4.** For beard, unbraid doll hair and cut into 3" lengths. Arranging beard as desired, glue beard along bottom ¹/₃ of face.

**5.** For glasses, refer to **Fig. 1** and bend wire as shown to fit face. Glue ends of wire to head. Glue hat to head.

**Fig. 1**

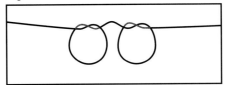

**6.** For placket on shirt, press long edges of fabric strip ¹/₂" to wrong side. Center and press fusible tape to wrong side of strip. Matching short ends of placket with long edges of shirt fabric, center placket on right side of shirt fabric; fuse in place. Topstitch close to long edges of placket to secure.

**7.** For shirt casing, press fusible tape along one long edge on wrong side of shirt fabric piece. Do not remove paper backing. Press edge 1³/₈" to wrong side; unfold edge and remove paper backing. Refold edge and fuse in place.

**8.** For shirt, press fusible tape to right side of one short edge of shirt fabric piece. Remove paper backing. Matching right sides and short edges, fuse edges together. Thread ribbon through opening in casing. Turn right side out. Spacing evenly, sew four buttons to placket.

**9.** For each sleeve, press one short edge of sleeve fabric piece 1¹/₂" to wrong side. Press fusible tape to right side of one long edge and remaining short raw edge. Remove paper backing. Matching right sides and raw edges, fuse edges together. Clip corners and turn right side out.

**10.** Insert one arm into one sleeve. With 2¹/₂" of arm extending past cuff of sleeve, fold cuff to form a pleat at wrist. Sew one button to sleeve over pleat. Tack sleeve to wrist. Repeat for remaining arm.

**11.** Hand sew head to casing at center front of shirt. Being careful not to catch ribbon in stitching, hand sew one sleeve to casing 2" from each side of placket.

**12.** With arms placed over basket handle, place shirt over top of basket. With bottom edge of shirt overlapping basket rim ¹/₂", glue edge of shirt to basket rim, easing to fit if necessary.

**13.** For belt, press edges of fabric strip ¹/₂" to wrong side. Overlapping ends at back, glue belt to rim of basket, covering raw edges of shirt.

**14.** Pull ribbon ends to close top of shirt; tie ends into a bow.

# PUFFY POINSETTIA BASKET

*Jazz up a gift of fresh Christmas flowers by presenting them in this pretty poinsettia basket. The cover is created by fusing red and green fabrics together. The cloth is gathered around a padded basket and embellished with a matching fabric bow.*

**You will need:**
Wonder-Under® transfer web
basket
red and green fabrics for bows,
    trim, and to cover basket
embroidery floss to match fabric
polyester fiberfill
four decorative wood buttons
fabric marking pencil
pinking shears
string
thumbtack
hot glue gun and glue sticks
pressing cloth

**1.** Measure basket from rim to rim (**Fig. 1**); add 6". Cut one square each from red and green fabric the determined measurement.

**Fig. 1**

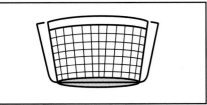

**2.** Measure around top of basket, add 1". Cut one strip each of red and green fabric 2" by the determined measurement for band and four strips 2" x 25" for bows.

**3.** Follow **Fusing Basics**, page 102, to fuse wrong sides of corresponding pieces of red and green fabrics together.

**4.** Using red and green square and measurement determined in Step 1, follow Step 2 of **Holiday Bath Basket**, page 80, to cut one circle. Use pinking shears to pink edges of circle, band, and all bow strips.

**5.** Use embroidery floss to baste 2¹/₂" from edge of circle. Follow Step 7 of **Holiday Bath Basket**, page 80, to gather and pad basket.

**6.** Glue gathers to top edge of basket.

**7.** For trim, glue band around gathers.

**8.** Using strips for bows, tie two red bows with green knots and two green bows with red knots.

**9.** Placing one bow over overlap of band and spacing remaining bows evenly around basket, glue bows to band.

**10.** Glue one button to knot of each bow.

# OLD-FASHIONED GOODIE BOXES

*These country-inspired containers will add old-fashioned style to the gifts you share!*
*To create them, plain Shaker boxes are painted in Christmasy colors and topped with giant*
*fabric yo-yos. A wooden heart and star and a twine bow are sweet finishing touches.*

**Note:** Supplies are for making one goodie box.

**You will need:**
Shaker-style box
fabrics for yo-yo and trim
items to decorate box (we used a 1$^1/_4$"w wooden star painted yellow, a 2$^1/_8$"w wooden heart sprayed with glossy wood tone spray, and a jute twine bow and a $^7/_8$" dia. button)
spray paint to coordinate with fabrics
fabric marking pencil
thread to match fabrics
string
thumbtack
hot glue gun and glue sticks

**1.** Spray paint box; allow to dry.

**2.** For yo-yo, measure diameter of box lid; multiply by 2. Cut a square of fabric the determined measurement.

**3.** Matching right sides, fold fabric square in half from top to bottom and again from left to right. Tie one end of string to fabric marking pencil. Measure $^1/_2$ the measurement determined in Step 2 from pencil; insert thumbtack through string at this point. Insert thumbtack through fabric as shown in **Fig. 1** and mark cutting line. Cutting through all layers, cut out circle.

**Fig. 1**

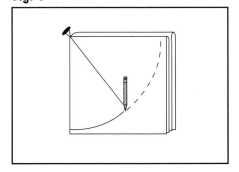

**4.** Turn edge of circle $^1/_4$" to wrong side and use a double strand of thread to baste along turned edge. Pull ends of thread to tightly gather circle; knot thread and trim ends. Flatten circle with gathers at center.

**5.** Glue yo-yo to top of box lid.

**6.** For trim, measure width of side of lid and add 1"; measure around lid and add 2". Cut a fabric strip the determined measurements. Press all edges $^1/_2$" to wrong side. Glue strip to side of lid, overlapping ends.

**7.** Decorate box lid as desired; glue items to secure.

# YULETIDE PHOTO ALBUMS

*Preserve Yuletide memories in one of these charming photo albums and then send the book to a family member who can't make it home for the holidays. The fabric-covered albums are decorated with torn-fabric strips, buttons, stars, and a joyous message.*

## Evergreen Album

**You will need:**
Wonder-Under® transfer web
7¹/₂"w x 12¹/₂"h x 2¹/₂"d album
fabric to cover album
green fabric for tree branches
fabric for braid trim
6" x 11" piece of muslin
10" x 23" piece of batting
two 7" x 11¹/₂" pieces of poster board
dark yellow and brown acrylic paint
small round paintbrush
assorted buttons
instant coffee
tracing paper
transfer paper
hot glue gun and glue sticks
pressing cloth

**1.** From fabric to cover album, cut the following pieces: one 16¹/₂" x 21¹/₂" piece for outside album cover, two 2" x 11¹/₂" strips, and two 9" x 13¹/₂" pieces for inside album covers.

**2.** With album closed, glue batting to outside of album.

**3.** Open album and center on wrong side of outside album cover fabric piece. Fold corners of fabric piece diagonally over corners of album; glue in place. Fold short edges of fabric over side edges of album; glue in place. Fold long edges of fabric over top and bottom edges of album, trimming fabric to fit ¹/₄" under binding hardware; glue in place.

**4.** Press short ends of each 2"w strip ¹/₄" to wrong side. Center and glue one strip along each side of binding hardware with one long edge of each strip tucked ¹/₄" under hardware.

**5.** Center one piece of poster board on wrong side of one inside album cover fabric piece. Fold corners of fabric diagonally over corners of poster board; glue in place. Fold edges of fabric over edges of cardboard; glue in place. Repeat to cover remaining poster board piece.

**6.** Center and glue wrong side of covered poster board pieces inside front and back covers of album.

**7.** Dissolve 2 tablespoons instant coffee in two cups hot water; allow to cool. Soak muslin in coffee several minutes; remove from coffee. Allow to dry and press.

**8.** Cut a 6" x 11" piece of web. Follow **Fusing Basics**, page 102, to center and press web to muslin piece. Center and fuse muslin piece on album front.

**9.** Trace tree trunk, tree topper, and beams patterns, page 138, onto tracing paper. Use transfer paper to transfer designs to center of muslin piece. Paint trunk brown and tree topper and beams dark yellow; allow to dry.

**10.** For tree branches, tear seven strips of various lengths and widths from tree branch fabric. Press strips of web to wrong side of each fabric strip. Arrange branches on tree trunk; fuse in place.

**11.** Sew a button to center of each branch.

**12.** Tear three 1" x 51" strips from braid fabric; braid strips. Glue braid around edges of muslin; trim excess.

## Yuletide Memories Album

**You will need:**
Wonder-Under® transfer web
10"w x 11¹/₂"h x 2"d album
fabric to cover album
assorted fabrics for appliqués
8" x 10" piece of muslin
10" x 23" piece of batting
two 9¹/₂" x 10¹/₂" pieces of poster board
dark green paint pen
brown permanent pen
assorted buttons
instant coffee
tracing paper
transfer paper
hot glue gun and glue sticks
pressing cloth

**1.** From fabric to cover album, cut the following pieces: one 15¹/₂" x 26" piece for outside album cover, two 11" x 12¹/₂" pieces for inside album covers, and two 2" x 10¹/₂" strips.

**2.** Using fabric pieces cut in Step 1, follow Steps 2 - 6 of **Evergreen Album** to cover album.

**3.** Dissolve 2 tablespoons instant coffee in two cups hot water; allow to cool. Soak muslin in coffee several minutes; remove from coffee. Allow to dry and press.

**4.** Cut a 7" x 9" piece of web. Follow **Fusing Basics**, page 102, to center and press web to muslin piece. Fringe edges of muslin to edges of web. Center and fuse muslin piece on album front.

**5.** Trace "Yuletide Memories" pattern, page 138, onto tracing paper. Use transfer paper to transfer design to center of muslin piece. Use green pen to draw over letters; allow to dry.

**6.** Using patterns, page 138, follow **Making Appliqués**, page 102, to make desired number of small star, medium star, and large star appliqués. Arrange appliqués on muslin; fuse in place.

**7.** Use brown pen to draw "stitches" around each star.

**8.** Glue buttons on album as desired.

# every nook & cranny

**H**ow wonderful and joyous it is to discover holiday reminders in unexpected places! A lighthearted afghan placed across a chair, a cheery grouping of throw pillows arranged in a cozy corner, or a frosty snow pal offering holiday greetings from a lampshade — each of these pieces can renew your Christmas spirit as you go about your day. And since they're crafted using creative shortcuts, you'll have even more time to enjoy your seasonal celebrations!

# GINGERBOY PILLOWS

*These cozy pillows are ideal for adding homey charm to a quiet corner.*
*The pillows are accented with gingerbread boy appliqués, which are lightly*
*padded with fiberfill and finished with buttons and blanket stitch embroidery.*

**Note:** Supplies are for making one pillow.

**You will need:**
- 8" x 10" piece of brown wool fabric
- 8" x 10" piece of fabric for background
- two 1⁷⁄₈" x 10" strips and two 1⁷⁄₈" x 8" strips of fabric for inner borders
- four 1⁷⁄₈" squares of fabric for corner squares
- two 1⁷⁄₈" x 12³⁄₄" strips and two 1⁷⁄₈" x 13¹⁄₂" strips of fabric for outer borders
- 13¹⁄₂" x 15¹⁄₂" piece of fabric for pillow back
- dark brown and black embroidery floss
- two ¹⁄₂" dia. buttons
- four ⁵⁄₈" dia. buttons
- polyester fiberfill
- thread to match fabrics
- tracing paper

**1.** Trace gingerboy pattern, page 139, onto tracing paper; cut out.

**2.** Use pattern to cut one gingerboy appliqué from brown wool.

**3.** For pillow top, center wrong side of gingerboy appliqué on right side of background fabric. Use three strands of dark brown floss to work **Blanket Stitch**, page 104, along edge of appliqué.

**4.** Cutting through background fabric only, cut a 2" opening in fabric behind gingerboy. Stuff lightly with fiberfill; sew opening closed by hand.

**5.** Use twelve strands of black floss to work a **French Knot**, page 105, for each eye. Sew ¹⁄₂" dia. buttons to front of gingerboy.

**6.** (**Note:** For all machine sewing, match right sides and raw edges and use a ¹⁄₄" seam allowance. Press seam allowances to one side.) For inner borders, sew 10" long strips to side edges of background. Sew one corner square to each short edge of each 8" long strip. Sew strips to top and bottom edges of background.

**7.** For outer borders, sew 12³⁄₄" long strips to side edges of inner border. Sew 13¹⁄₂" long strips to top and bottom edges of inner border.

**8.** Sew one ⁵⁄₈" dia. button to each corner square.

**9.** Place pillow top and back right sides together. Leaving an opening for turning, sew front and back together. Clip corners, turn right side out, and press. Stuff with fiberfill and sew final closure by hand.

# CROCHETED STAR RUG

*This country star rug shines with holiday cheer. Crocheted with fabric strips*
*and a large hook, the holiday accent can be worked up in a twinkling!*

**You will need:**
- 5 yds **each** of 44/45"w red, green, and gold 100% cotton fabrics
- crochet hook, size P
- yarn needle

**Note:** Follow **Preparing Fabric Strips**, page 104, to tear fabric into 1¹⁄₂"w fabric strips. Read **Crochet**, page 103, before beginning project.

**DIAMOND** (make 6)
**First Side**
Ch 21 **loosely**.

**Row 1:** Sc in second ch from hook and in each ch across: 20 sc.

**Row 2** (Right side): Turn; skip first sc, slip st in next sc, sc in next 16 sc, leave last 2 sc unworked: 16 sc.

**Note:** Loop a short piece of fabric around any stitch to mark last row as **right** side.

**Row 3:** Turn; skip first sc, slip st in next sc, sc in next 12 sc, leave remaining 2 sc unworked: 12 sc.

**Row 4:** Turn; skip first sc, slip st in next sc, sc in next 8 sc, leave remaining 2 sc unworked: 8 sc.

**Row 5:** Turn; skip first sc, slip st in next sc, sc in next 4 sc, leave remaining 2 sc unworked: 4 sc.

**Row 6:** Turn; skip first sc, sc in next 2 sc, leave remaining sc unworked; finish off.

**Second Side**
**Row 1:** With **wrong** side facing and working in free loops of beginning ch (**Fig. 1**), join fabric with slip st in first ch; ch 1, sc in same st and in each ch across: 20 sc.

**Fig. 1**

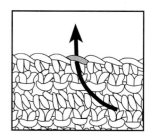

FINISHING

## Assembly

Using photo as a guide for placement, whipstitch rug together as follows:

With **wrong** sides of two Diamonds together and working in inside loops, insert needle from **right** to **left** through one st on **each** piece (**Fig. 2**).

**Fig. 2**

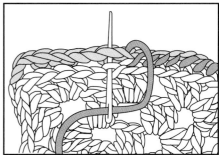

Bring needle around and insert from **right** to **left** through next st on **both** pieces.

Continue in this manner, keeping sewing fabric fairly loose.

Whipstitch remaining Diamonds to form a star. Whipstitch Half Diamonds between 2 points of Star, leaving first and last sc on Half Diamond unworked; then sew side edges of Half Diamonds together.

### Trim

With **right** side facing and working in free loops of beginning ch of Half Diamonds and in joinings, join fabric with slip st in first ch of any Half Diamond; ch 1, 2 sc in same st, sc in next 5 chs, 2 sc in next ch, sc in next 6 chs, 2 sc in next ch, sc in next 5 chs, 2 sc in next ch, sc in next joining, ch 2, sc in top of sc just made, H 2 sc in next ch, sc in next 5 chs, 2 sc in next ch, sc in next 6 chs, 2 sc in next ch, sc in next 5 chs, 2 sc in next ch, sc in next joining, ch 2, sc in top of sc just made; repeat from H around; join with slip st to first sc, finish off.

**Rows 2 - 6:** Work same as First Side; do **not** finish off.

### Edging

Ch 1, do **not** turn; work 11 sc evenly spaced across to beginning ch; (sc, hdc, sc) in same ch as sc (end of beginning ch); work 12 sc evenly spaced across to Row 6, (sc, hdc, sc) in first sc; work 12 sc evenly spaced across to beginning ch, (sc, hdc, sc) in same ch as sc (end of beginning ch); work 12 sc evenly spaced across to Row 6; (sc, hdc, sc) in first sc, sc in next sc; join with slip st to first sc, finish off.

### HALF DIAMOND (make 6)

Work same as First Side of Diamond.

### Edging

With **right** side facing, join fabric with slip st in end of Row 1; ch 1, work 15 sc evenly spaced across to Row 6; (sc, hdc, sc) in first sc, work 15 sc evenly spaced across to beginning ch; finish off.

# PLACE MAT COVER-UP

*Here's a quick-and-clever way to dress up your holiday table — simply slip your everyday vinyl place mat into our jolly gingerbread men cover-up! Each of the happy-faced fellows is fused in place and accented with a tiny bow tie and button.*

**You will need:**
Wonder-Under® transfer web
11¹/₂" x 17¹/₄" vinyl place mat
15¹/₂" x 25" piece of fabric
1¹/₂" x 25" strip of fabric for narrow trim
7" x 25" strip of fabric for wide trim
assorted fabrics for appliqués
three 7" lengths of ¹/₈"w satin ribbon
three ¹/₂" dia. buttons
thread to match fabrics
black permanent pen
pressing cloth

**Note:** For all machine stitching, use a ¹/₂" seam allowance and press seam allowances open.

**1.** Matching wrong sides and long edges, press wide trim in half.

**2.** Matching long raw edges of wide trim to right side and one long edge of narrow trim, sew trim pieces together to make border.

**3.** Matching long raw edges, sew border and 15¹/₂" x 25" fabric piece together for cover.

**4.** Matching right sides and short edges, sew long edges of cover together. Do not turn right side out. Press cover flat with seam at center back. Sew remaining raw edges together. Clip corners diagonally and turn right side out; press.

**5.** Using patterns, page 139, follow **Making Appliqués**, page 102, to make three each of gingerbread man and gingerbread man background appliqués.

**6.** Arrange appliqués on right side of border, overlapping as necessary; fuse in place.

**7.** Use pen to draw eyes and mouth on each gingerbread man.

**8.** Tie each ribbon length into a bow. Sew one bow and one button to each gingerbread man.

**9.** Insert vinyl place mat into cover.

# SNOWMAN AFGHAN

*As our winsome snowman plays with a jump rope of stars, he's sure to bring a smile to your face. For a fast finish, the fanciful design is fused onto an Anne Cloth afghan and then embellished with blanket stitching and buttons. Simple running stitches accent the coordinating binding, which is fused around the edges.*

**Fig. 1**

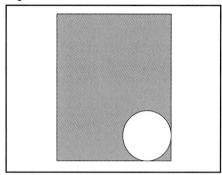

**3.** (**Note:** When making binding, add an additional 10" to length for tie.) Follow **Binding**, page 102, to add 2¹/₂"w fused binding to edges of afghan.

**4.** Using patterns, page 140, follow **Making Appliqués**, page 102, to make one snowman and two (one in reverse) arm appliqués from cotton batting; three each of patch and large star appliqués, two (one in reverse) mitten appliqués, and one each of hat and hat trim appliqués from fabrics; and one scarf appliqué from binding fabric.

**5.** Arrange all appliqués except stars on one corner of afghan, overlapping as necessary; fuse in place.

**6.** Use three strands of cream floss to work **Running Stitch**, page 105, along binding. Leaving a 1¹/₂" tail on each mitten, work **Running Stitch** "jump rope" between mittens. Knot both ends of floss. Arrange and fuse stars along "rope."

**7.** Use three strands of black floss to work **Blanket Stitch**, page 104, around each appliqué. For tie, cut a 9" length from remaining binding. Use three strands of floss to work **Blanket Stitch** along open edges of tie. Knot tie at center and tack to scarf at neck; tack "jump rope" ends to mittens.

**8.** Sew ¹/₄" dia. buttons to face for eyes and remaining buttons to body.

**You will need:**
Heavy Duty Wonder-Under® transfer web
Wonder-Under® fusible tape
45" x 58" piece of Anne Cloth
cotton batting for snowman
assorted fabrics for appliqués
fabric for binding, scarf, and tie
cream and black embroidery floss
two ¹/₄" dia. black buttons for eyes
three assorted black buttons for body
small plate or saucer
pressing cloth

**1.** (**Note:** To reduce fraying, hand wash and line dry Anne Cloth.) Wash, dry, and press fabrics.

**2.** To round corners of Anne Cloth, place plate on one corner of fabric as shown in **Fig. 1**. Draw around curve of plate; cut along drawn line. Repeat for remaining corners.

# KRIS KRINGLE PILLOW

*Complete your seasonal decor with this fun throw pillow featuring the jolly old elf! The welted
cushion has a fused-on appliqué of Kris Kringle sharing his wishes for a "Merry Christmas."*

## You will need:

Wonder-Under® transfer web
11" x 12" piece of fabric for
    background
four 1¹/₄" x 13¹/₂" strips of fabric
    for inner borders
four 2³/₄" x 17¹/₂" strips of fabric
    for outer borders
18" x 19" piece of fabric for pillow
    back
assorted fabrics for appliqués
fabric strip for welting
fusible interfacing (optional)
tear-away stabilizer
¹/₂" dia. cord for welting
polyester fiberfill
clear nylon thread
pink, red, green, and black
    permanent fabric pens
pressing cloth

**Note:** For all machine sewing, match
right sides and raw edges and use a
¹/₄" seam allowance. Press seam
allowances to one side (toward the
darker fabric whenever possible).

**1.** Trimming off remainder of each
border after stitching, sew one inner
border to each 12" edge (top/bottom)
of background. Sew one inner border
to each side edge of background.
Repeat to add outer borders to make
pillow top.

**2.** Using patterns, pages 122, 123,
and 139, follow **Making Appliqués**,
page 102, to make one each of coat,
coat trim, face, beard, mustache, cap,
cap trim, grass, and banner
appliqués; two each of tree trunk,
medium tree, and large star
appliqués; two (one in reverse) each
of cuff, boot, and glove appliqués;
and four small star appliqués.

**3.** Arrange appliqués on pillow top,
overlapping as necessary; fuse in
place. Use clear thread and follow
**Machine Appliqué**, page 105, to stitch
over raw edges of appliqués.

**4.** Use pens to write "Merry
Christmas" and draw holly leaves,
berries, and border design on banner;
draw eyes and nose on face; and
"stitches" on beard and mustache.

**5.** For welting, measure around edges
of pillow; add 2". Cut a length of cord
and a 3¹/₂"w bias strip of fabric the
determined measurement.

**6.** Press one end of bias strip ¹/₂" to
wrong side. Center cord on wrong
side of bias strip. Matching long
edges, fold strip over cord. Using
zipper foot, baste along length of strip
close to cord; trim seam allowance to
¹/₂". Beginning with pressed end of
welting at center bottom of pillow front

and matching raw edges, pin welting
to right side of pillow front, clipping
seam allowance at corners. Overlap
ends of welting 1" and trim excess.
Remove basting from 1" of pressed
end of welting and trim ends of cord
to fit. Overlap pressed end of fabric
over unfinished end of welting. Baste
ends in place.

**7.** Place pillow front and back right
sides together. Stitching as close as
possible to welting and leaving an
opening for turning, use zipper foot to
sew front and back together. Clip
corners, turn right side out, and press.
Stuff with fiberfill and sew final closure
by hand.

# WINTRY LAMPSHADE

*Charming country fabrics and simple buttons transform a purchased lampshade kit into a sweet holiday conversation piece. Featuring a fused-on snowman and a "forest" of evergreens, the cute design will brighten any little nook with wintry appeal.*

**You will need:**
Wonder-Under® transfer web
self-adhesive lampshade kit
fabric to cover lampshade
assorted fabrics for appliqués
black embroidery floss
two ¹/₂" dia. red buttons
large-eye needle
black permanent pen
tracing paper
fabric glue
pressing cloth

**1.** For lampshade, use pattern provided with kit to cut one piece from lampshade fabric. Do not apply to shade.

**2.** Using patterns, page 141, follow **Making Appliqués**, page 102, to make two each of large tree, medium tree, small tree, and dot (one for pom-pom and one for bow tie knot) appliqués; two (one in reverse) of mitten appliqués, and one each of snowman, cap, cap trim, nose, streamer A, streamer B, and bow tie appliqués.

**3.** Arrange appliqués on right side of lampshade fabric, overlapping as necessary; fuse in place.

**4.** Use pen to draw eyes and mouth on face. Using six strands of floss, pull one end of floss through center of one mitten; knot floss on wrong side of fabric. Pull opposite end of floss through remaining mitten. Adjust floss to desired tension and knot floss on wrong side of fabric; trim ends. Sew buttons to snowman.

**5.** Trace heart, star A, and star B patterns, page 141, onto tracing paper; cut out.

**6.** Use patterns to cut one each of heart, star A, and star B from fabric. Glue shapes along floss; allow to dry.

**7.** Use pen to draw "stitches" along outside edge of snowman and all tree appliqués.

**8.** Follow lampshade kit instructions to adhere lampshade fabric to lampshade. Use pen to draw "stitches" ¹/₄" from top and bottom edges of shade.

95

# QUICK CHAIR ACCENT

*Add holiday flair to a straight-back chair with our colorful chairback cover! The cheery accent is easy to make because the hems and appliqués are fused in place.*

**You will need:**
Wonder-Under® transfer web
Wonder-Under® fusible tape
12" x 28" piece of fabric for chairback cover
16$\frac{1}{2}$" x 32$\frac{1}{2}$" piece of fabric for borders
four 1$\frac{1}{2}$" x 16" strips of fabric for ties
assorted fabrics for appliqués
assorted buttons
pressing cloth

**1.** Cut a 2$\frac{1}{4}$" square from each corner of border fabric piece (**Fig. 1**).

**Fig. 1**

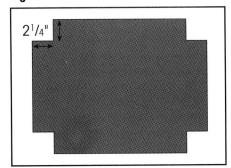

**2.** Follow **Fusing Basics**, page 102, to press web to wrong side of chairback cover fabric piece. Center cover on border fabric piece; fuse in place.

**3.** Press one short edge of border fabric piece $\frac{3}{4}$" to wrong side. Press fusible tape along pressed edge; do not remove paper backing. Press edge 1$\frac{1}{2}$" to wrong side, covering edge of chairback cover (**Fig. 2**). Unfold edge and remove paper backing. Refold and fuse in place. Repeat for remaining short edge.

**Fig. 2**

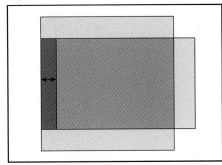

**4.** Press one unfused corner of border fabric piece diagonally to wrong side (**Fig. 3**). Press a piece of fusible tape along diagonal edge (**Fig. 4**); do not remove paper backing. Repeat for remaining corners.

**Fig. 3**

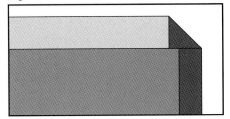

**Fig. 4**

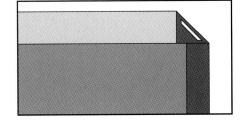

**5.** Press long edge of border fabric piece $\frac{3}{4}$" to wrong side. Press fusible tape along pressed edge; do not remove paper backing. Press edge 1$\frac{1}{2}$" to wrong side, covering edge of chairback cover. Unfold edge and remove paper backing from all edges. Refold edge and fuse in place. Repeat for remaining edge of border fabric piece.

**6.** Using patterns, page 142, follow **Making Appliqués**, page 102, to make one each of tree A, tree B, tree C, and small tree trunk appliqués; two large tree trunk appliqués; and desired number of star appliqués.

**7.** Arrange appliqués on chairback cover, overlapping as necessary; fuse in place.

**8.** For ties, fold short, then long edges of fabric strips $\frac{3}{8}$" to wrong side; press. Press fusible tape to wrong side of strips. Matching wrong sides and long edges, fold each strip in half and fuse together.

**9.** Mark a dot on one corner of chairback cover 2$\frac{1}{4}$" from short edge and $\frac{1}{2}$" from long edge for tie/button placement (**Fig. 5**). With button on right side of cover and tie on wrong side, sew one end of tie and one button to cover. Repeat to add remaining ties.

**Fig. 5**

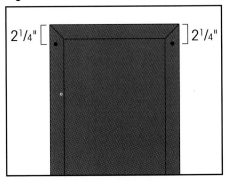

**10.** Sew additional buttons to cover as desired.

# NINE-PATCH MANTEL SCARF

*Draped with our simple Nine-Patch mantel scarf, your fireplace will glow with rustic charm. The runner is especially carefree to assemble because the blocks are fused together. And there's no binding — just sew the front and back pieces together with a layer of batting and then turn the scarf right side out! Machine quilting makes it fast to finish.*

**You will need:**
Wonder-Under® transfer web
two pieces of light tan print fabric
    for scarf front and back
assorted light and dark print fabrics
    for Nine-Patch appliqués
cotton batting
clear nylon thread
template material
black permanent pen
removable fabric marking pen
pressing cloth

**1.** Measure length and width of mantel as shown in **Fig. 1**. Round length measurement down to a number divisible by $8^1/2$" to determine finished length for scarf; add $^1/2$". Add $8^1/2$" to width measurement. Cut scarf front and scarf back the determined measurements from light tan print.

**Fig. 1**

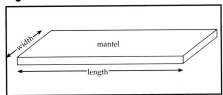

**2.** Divide finished length measurement (determined in Step 1) by $8^1/2$" to determine the number of Nine-Patch blocks to make.

**3.** Using removable pen, draw a line across length of fabric piece $4^1/2$" from one long edge (**Fig. 2**).

**Fig. 2**

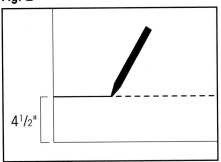

$4^1/2$"

**4.** Use permanent pen to trace triangle pattern, page 106, onto template material. Transfer dashed placement lines onto template; cut out.

**5.** Place template on scarf front, aligning long edge of template with line drawn on scarf front and matching right and lower points of template with raw edge of scarf front (**Fig. 3**). Draw around bottom edges of template below placement line.

**Fig. 3**

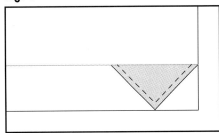

**6.** Placing template along drawn line on scarf front and overlapping seam allowance, continue to draw around template below placement line the number of times determined in Step 2 (**Fig. 4**).

**Fig. 4**

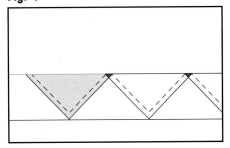

**7.** Cut out scarf front along drawn points without cutting into seam allowances.

**8.** Place scarf back right side up on batting. Matching right sides, place scarf front wrong side up on scarf back; pin layers together. Using scarf front as pattern, trim batting and backing even with raw edges of scarf front.

**9.** Leaving a 6" opening for turning and using a $^1/4$" seam allowance, sew scarf front, scarf back, and batting together. Clip corners and inside angles, turn right side out, and press. Sew final closure by hand.

**10.** Follow **Fusing Basics**, page 102, to press web to wrong side of light and dark print fabrics for Nine-Patch blocks.

**11.** For each Nine-Patch block, cut one 6" square from a light print fabric and five 2" squares from a coordinating dark print fabric. Do not remove paper backing from 6" square. Arrange 2" squares on 6" square and fuse in place.

**12.** Arrange blocks on scarf front and fuse in place.

**13.** Using **Quilting Diagram** as a suggestion, use removable pen to mark quilting lines.

**14.** Use clear thread to machine stitch along marked lines to quilt mantel scarf.

**Quilting Diagram**

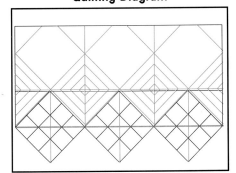

*Show your holiday spirit with this starry Christmas table runner! Created using a no-sew strip-piecing method, the runner can also be spread across the table to serve as two place mats.*

**You will need:**
Wonder-Under® transfer web
Wonder-Under® fusible tape
16" x 61" piece of fabric for table runner
6" x 58" piece of fabric for outer borders
$4^{1}/_{2}$" x $54^{3}/_{4}$" piece of fabric for inner borders
four $4^{1}/_{2}$" squares of fabric for block appliqués
assorted fabrics for star appliqués
assorted buttons
tracing paper
hot glue gun and glue sticks
pressing cloth

**1.** Wash, dry, and press fabrics.

**2.** Follow **Fusing Basics**, page 102, to press fusible tape along each long edge on wrong side of 16" x 61" fabric piece. Fold each edge $1/2$" to wrong side; fuse in place. Repeat for each short edge.

**3.** Press web to wrong side of outer border, inner border, and block appliqué fabric pieces. Do not remove paper backing.

**4.** For outer border, cut two $1^{1}/_{4}$" x 58" strips and two $1^{1}/_{4}$" x $13^{1}/_{2}$" strips from outer border fabric piece. Remove paper backing. Center each 58" strip $3/4$" from each long edge of table runner; fuse in place. Center each $13^{1}/_{2}$" strip 1" from each short edge, overlapping ends of long strips (**Fig. 1**); fuse in place.

**Fig. 1**

**5.** For block appliqués, cut two $1^{1}/_{2}$" x 3" pieces from each block fabric. Remove paper backing. Place four blocks 4" from one short edge of table runner, overlapping as necessary (**Fig. 2**); fuse in place. Repeat for remaining end of table runner.

**Fig. 2**

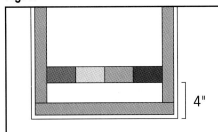

4"

**6.** For inner border, cut two $3/4$" x $54^{3}/_{4}$" strips and four $3/4$" x 11" strips from inner border fabric piece. Remove paper backing. Place one 11" strip 6" from one short edge of table runner (**Fig. 3**); fuse in place. Repeat for remaining short edge of table runner.

**Fig. 3**

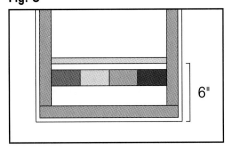

6"

**7.** Center one $54^{3}/_{4}$" strip along inner edge of each side outer border; fuse in place. Place remaining 11" strips $2^{5}/_{8}$" from each short edge, overlapping ends of long strips (**Fig. 4**); fuse in place.

**Fig. 4**

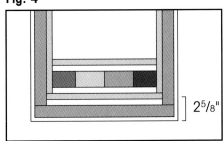

$2^{5}/_{8}$"

**8.** Using star pattern, follow **Making Appliqués**, page 102, to make six star appliqués, cutting some in reverse, if desired.

**9.** Arrange stars on each end of table runner; fuse in place.

**10.** Glue one button to center of each block and star appliqué.

Star

## PELLON® WONDER-UNDER® TRANSFER WEB AND FUSIBLE TAPE

Original weight Wonder-Under® and Heavy Duty Wonder-Under® are both available by the yard and in a 3/4"w pre-cut tape. Heavy Duty Wonder-Under® is recommended for use on heavier fabrics such as denim, canvas, and felt and to create a stronger bond between fabrics when omitting stitching around appliqués.

### Fusing Basics

**1.** Place web side of Wonder-Under® on wrong side of fabric. Press for five seconds with hot, dry iron. Let cool. (**Note:** If Wonder-Under® sticks to iron, it can be removed using a hot iron cleaner, available at fabric and craft stores.)

**2.** Remove paper backing.

**3.** Position fusible fabric, web side down, on project. Fusible items can be held temporarily in place by "touch basting." Touch item to be fused with tip of iron only. If item is not in desired position, it can be lifted and repositioned.

**4.** To fuse, cover fabric with damp pressing cloth. Using iron heated to wool setting, press firmly for ten seconds. (**Note:** Heavier fabrics require more time.) Repeat, lifting and overlapping iron until all fabric is fused.

**5.** Remove pressing cloth and iron fabric to eliminate excess moisture.

### Making Appliqués

To prevent darker fabrics from showing through, white or light-colored fabrics may need to be lined with fusible interfacing before applying Wonder-Under® transfer web.

To make reverse appliqué pieces, trace pattern onto tracing paper; turn traced pattern over and continue to follow all steps using reversed pattern.

When an appliqué pattern contains shaded areas, trace along entire outer line for appliqué indicated in project instructions. Trace outer lines of shaded areas for additional appliqués indicated in project instructions.

**1.** Use a pencil to trace pattern onto paper side of Wonder-Under® as many times as indicated in project instructions for a single fabric. Repeat for additional patterns and fabrics.

**2.** Follow Step 1 of **Fusing Basics** to press traced patterns to wrong side of fabrics. Do not remove paper backing.

**3.** Cut out appliqué pieces along traced lines.

**4.** Follow project instructions and Steps 2 - 5 of **Fusing Basics** to fuse appliqués to project.

### Foil Method

When applying Wonder-Under® transfer web to narrow items or items with holes, such as ribbon, lace, or doilies, it is necessary to place a piece of foil under the items to prevent web from adhering to your pressing surface.

**1.** Place a large piece of aluminum foil, shiny side up, on ironing board. Place item(s) to be made into appliqué(s), wrong side up, on foil.

**2.** Lay a piece of web or fusible tape, paper side up, over item(s). Follow Step 1 of **Fusing Basics** to press web to item(s); remove paper backing. Peel item(s) from foil and trim excess web.

**3.** Follow project instructions and Steps 2 - 5 of **Fusing Basics** to fuse appliqués to project.

## BINDING
### Making Binding

**1.** To determine length of binding strip needed, measure edges of item to be bound; add 12" to measurement. For clothing, begin at one lower front edge and measure along front, neckline, and bottom edges and around each sleeve (**Fig. 1**); add 12" to measurement.

**Fig. 1**

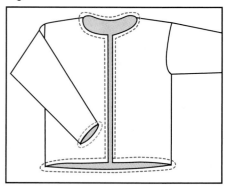

**2.** To give binding flexibility to fit around corners and curved edges, cut fabric strips on the bias. Cut bias strips the width indicated in project instructions and piece as necessary for determined length.

### Adding Sewn Binding

**1.** Matching wrong sides and raw edges, press binding strip in half lengthwise.

**2.** Press one end of binding strip diagonally (**Fig. 2**).

**Fig. 2**

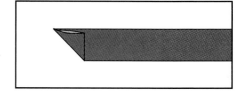

**3.** Beginning with pressed end several inches from a corner, pin binding to right side of item along one edge.

**4.** When first corner is reached, mark 1/4" from corner of item (**Fig. 3**).

**Fig. 3**

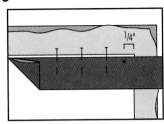

**5.** Using a 1/4" seam allowance, sew binding to item, backstitching at beginning and when mark is reached (**Fig. 4**). Lift needle and clip thread.

**Fig. 4**

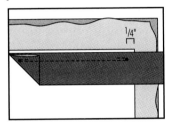

**6.** Fold binding as shown in **Figs. 5** and **6** and pin binding to adjacent side, matching raw edges. Mark 1/4" from edge of item at next corner.

**Fig. 5**

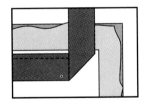

**Fig. 6**

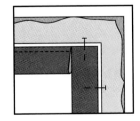

**7.** Backstitching at edge of binding, sew pinned binding to item (**Fig. 7**); backstitch when next mark is reached. Lift needle and clip thread.

**Fig. 7**

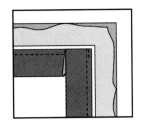

**8.** Repeat Steps 6 and 7 to continue sewing binding to item until binding overlaps beginning end by 2". Trim excess binding.

**9.** If binding a quilt, trim backing and batting even with quilt top edge.

**10.** For a mitered corner, fold binding over to backing of item and pin pressed edge in place, covering stitching line (**Fig. 8**). Fold adjacent edge over to backing of item, forming a mitered corner (**Fig. 9**), and pin in place. Repeat for each corner.

**Fig. 8**

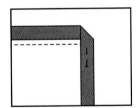

**Fig. 9**

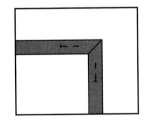

**11.** Hand sew binding to backing, taking care not to stitch through front of item.

# Adding Fused Binding

**1.** With wrong sides together, press fabric strip in half lengthwise; unfold. With wrong sides together, press long raw edges to center.

**2.** Follow Step 1 of **Fusing Basics** to press fusible tape along each pressed edge on wrong side of binding; do not remove paper backing.

**3.** Press binding in half lengthwise again. Unfold binding and remove paper backing.

**4.** Working around item and mitering corners as necessary, insert raw edges of item into fold of binding. Follow Steps 2 - 5 of **Fusing Basics** to fuse binding in place as you work around item. Do not fuse loose end over beginning end.

**5.** Trim loose end 1" past beginning end. Press loose end 1/2" to wrong side. Overlap pressed end over beginning end; fuse in place. Use fabric glue to secure loose fabric at corners and end of binding; allow to dry.

# CROCHET
## Abbreviations

| | |
|---|---|
| ch(s) | chain(s) |
| hdc | half double crochet(s) |
| mm | millimeters |
| Rnd(s) | Round(s) |
| sc | single crochet(s) |
| sp(s) | space(s) |
| st(s) | stitch(es) |
| YO | yarn over |

★ — work instructions following ★ as many **more** times as indicated in addition to the first time.

( ) — work enclosed instructions **as many** times as specified by the number immediately following **or** work all enclosed instructions in the stitch or space indicated **or** contains explanatory remarks.

## Gauge

When crocheting with fabric strips, gauge does not really matter; the finished piece can be slightly larger or smaller without changing the overall effect. However, even tension must be maintained throughout to keep the piece flat.

## Single Crochet

Insert hook in stitch or space indicated, YO and pull up a loop, YO and draw through both loops on hook (**Fig. 1**).

Fig. 1

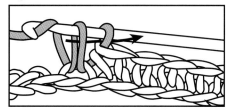

## Half Double Crochet

YO, insert hook in stitch or space indicated, YO and pull up a loop, YO and draw through all three loops on hook (**Fig. 2**).

Fig. 2

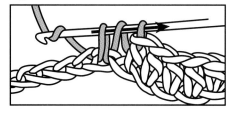

## Preparing Fabric Strips

**1.** Wash, dry, and press fabrics; tear off selvages. Tear fabric into strips at least two yards long by the width indicated in project instructions.

**2.** To join a new strip of fabric to working strip, cut a ¹/₂" slit about ¹/₂" from ends of both fabric strips (**Fig 3**).

Fig. 3

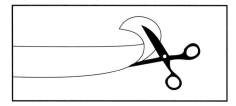

**3.** With right sides up, place end of new strip over end of working strip and match slits (**Fig. 4**).

Fig. 4

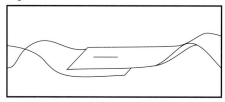

**4.** Pull free end of new strip through both slits from bottom to top (**Fig. 5**).

Fig. 5

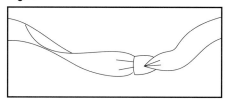

**5.** Pull new strip firmly to form a small knot (**Fig. 6**). Right sides of both strips should be facing up. Continue working with new strip.

Fig. 6

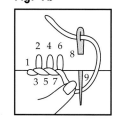

# EMBROIDERY STITCHES
## Blanket Stitch

Bring needle up at 1; keeping thread below point of needle, go down at 2 and come up at 3 (**Fig. 1a**). Continue working as shown in **Fig. 1b**.

Fig. 1a          Fig. 1b

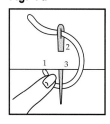 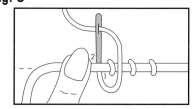

## Chain Stitch

Bring needle up at 1; take needle down again at 1 to form a loop and bring needle up at 2 (**Fig. 2a**). Take needle down again at 2 to form a loop and bring needle up at 3 (**Fig. 2b**). Continue as shown in **Fig. 2c**. To finish row of stitches, keep floss below point of needle; take needle down at 6 to anchor loop.

Fig. 2a          Fig. 2b

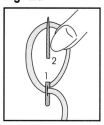 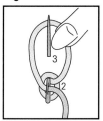

Fig. 2c

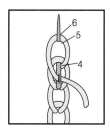

## Couching Stitch

Thread first needle with desired number of threads or cord to be couched and bring up through fabric. Hold threads or cord along desired line. Using a second needle, bring couching thread up at 1 and down at 2 to secure laid threads or cord (**Fig. 3**). Repeat to secure threads or cord along desired line.

Fig. 3

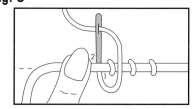

## Cross Stitch

Bring needle up at 1 and go down at 2. Come up at 3 and go down at 4 (**Fig. 4**).

**Fig. 4**

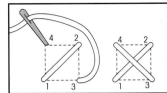

## French Knot

Bring needle up at 1. Wrap floss once around needle and insert needle at 2, holding end of floss with non-stitching fingers (**Fig. 5**). Tighten knot, then pull needle through fabric, holding floss until it must be released. For larger knot, use more strands of floss; wrap only once.

**Fig. 5**

## Running Stitch

Make a series of straight stitches with stitch length equal to the space between stitches (**Fig. 6**).

**Fig. 6**

## Stem Stitch

Referring to **Fig. 7**, bring needle up at 1; keeping thread below the stitching line, go down at 2 and bring needle up at 3. Take needle down at 4 and bring needle up at 5.

**Fig. 7**

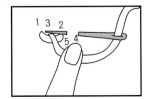

## Straight Stitch

Bring needle up at 1 and go down at 2 (**Fig. 8**). Length of stitches may be varied as desired.

**Fig. 8**

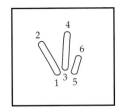

# MACHINE APPLIQUÉ

Unless otherwise indicated in project instructions, set sewing machine for a medium-width zigzag stitch with a short stitch length. When using nylon or metallic thread for appliqué, use regular thread in bobbin.

**1.** Pin or baste a piece of stabilizer slightly larger than design to wrong side of background fabric under design.

**2.** Beginning on straight edge of appliqué if possible, position fabric under presser foot so that most of stitching will be on appliqué piece. Holding upper thread toward you, sew over thread for two or three stitches to prevent thread from raveling. Stitch over all exposed raw edges of appliqué(s) and along detail lines as indicated in project instructions.

**3.** When stitching is complete, remove stabilizer. Pull loose threads to wrong side of fabric; knot and trim ends.

# QUILTING

Thread quilting needle with an 18" to 20" length of quilting thread; knot one end. Using a thimble, insert needle into quilt top and batting approximately $1/2$" from first stitch. When knot catches on quilt top, give thread a short, quick pull to pop knot through fabric into batting (**Fig. 1**). To quilt, use a small **Running Stitch** (**Fig. 2**) to stitch through all layers. At end of thread length, knot thread close to fabric and pop knot into batting. Clip thread close to fabric.

**Fig. 1**

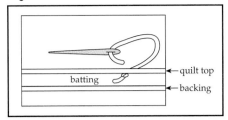

**Fig. 2**

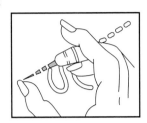

# SEWING SHAPES

**1.** Center pattern on wrong side of one fabric piece; use fabric marking pencil or pen to draw around pattern. Do not cut out shape.

**2.** Place fabric pieces right sides together. Leaving an opening for turning, carefully sew pieces together directly on drawn line.

**3.** Leaving a $1/4$" seam allowance, cut out shape. Clip seam allowance at curves and corners. Turn right side out and press.

# TRACING PATTERNS

**When entire pattern is shown**, place tracing paper over pattern and trace pattern; cut out. For a more durable pattern, use a permanent pen to trace pattern onto template material; cut out.

**When only half of pattern is shown (indicated by blue line on pattern)**, fold tracing paper in half and place fold along blue line of pattern. Trace pattern half; turn folded paper over and draw over traced lines on remaining side of paper. Unfold paper and cut out pattern. For a more durable pattern, use a permanent pen to trace pattern half onto template material; turn template material over and align blue lines to form a whole pattern. Trace pattern half again; cut out.

# USING DIMENSIONAL PAINT

**Note:** Before painting on garment, practice painting on scrap fabric.

**1.** To keep paint flowing smoothly, turn bottle upside down and allow paint to fill tip of bottle before each use.

**2.** Clean tip often with a paper towel.

**3.** If tip becomes clogged, insert a straight pin into tip opening.

**4.** When painting lines or painting over appliqués, keep bottle tip in contact with fabric, applying a thick line of paint centered over drawn line or raw edge of appliqué.

**5.** To correct a mistake, use a paring knife to gently scrape excess paint from fabric before it dries. Carefully remove stain with non-acetone nail polish remover. A mistake may also be camouflaged by incorporating the mistake into the design.

**6.** Keep garment lying flat for at least 24 hours to ensure that paint is sufficiently set before adding additional trims.

## Adding Glitter To Paint

**1.** Follow **Using Dimensional Paint** to paint all areas that will not be covered with glitter; allow to dry.

**2.** Paint glitter appliqué as indicated in project instructions. Generously sprinkle glitter on paint; allow to dry.

**3.** Shake excess glitter from garment.

**4.** Repeat as necessary.

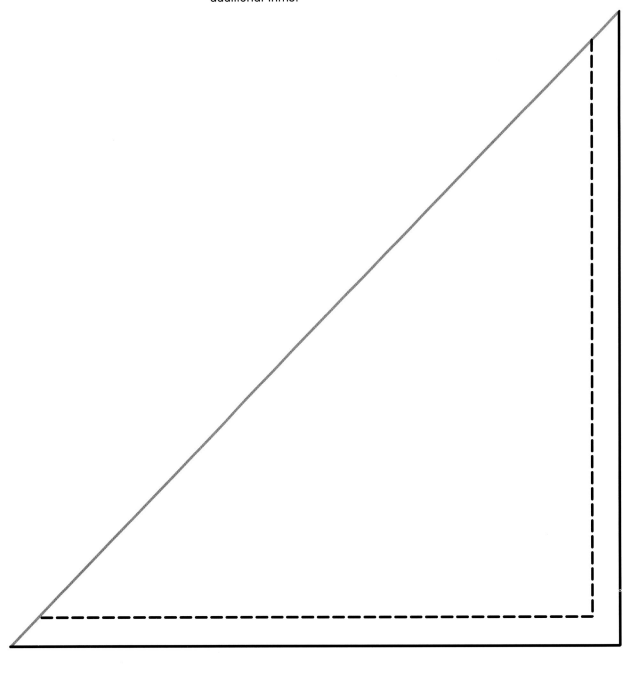

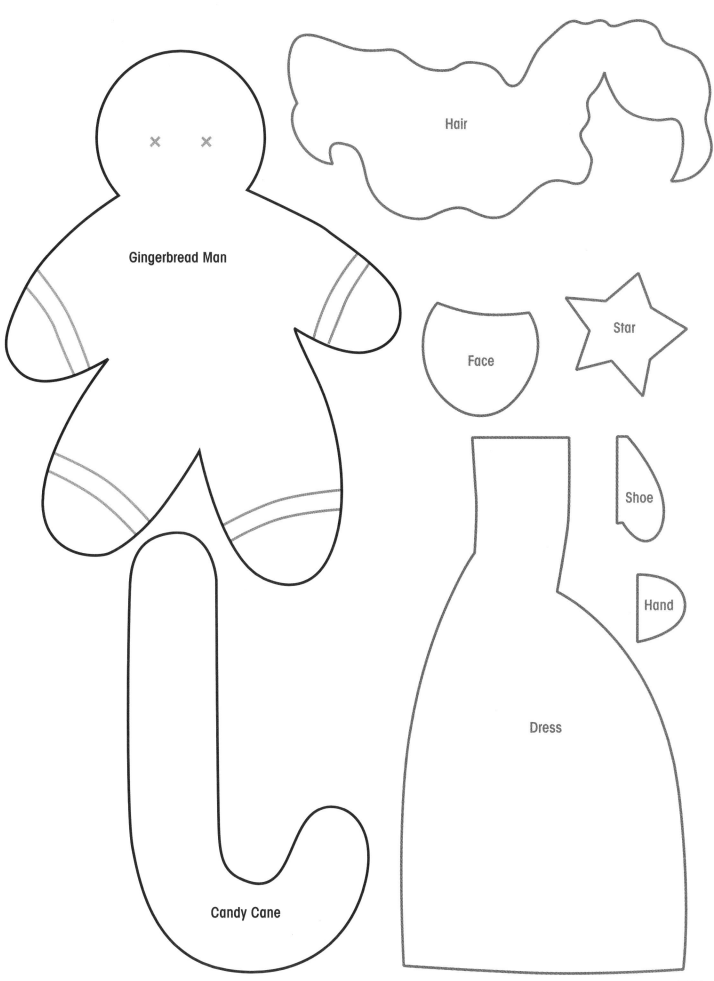

Gingerbread Man

Hair

Face

Star

Shoe

Hand

Dress

Candy Cane

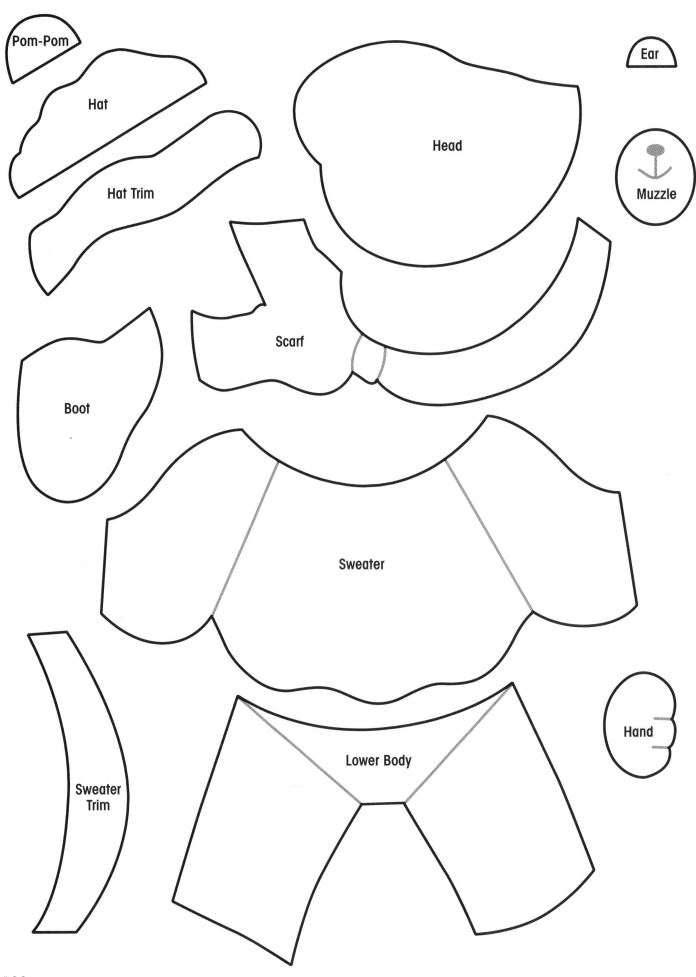

Pom-Pom

Hat

Hat Trim

Ear

Head

Muzzle

Boot

Scarf

Sweater

Sweater Trim

Lower Body

Hand

108

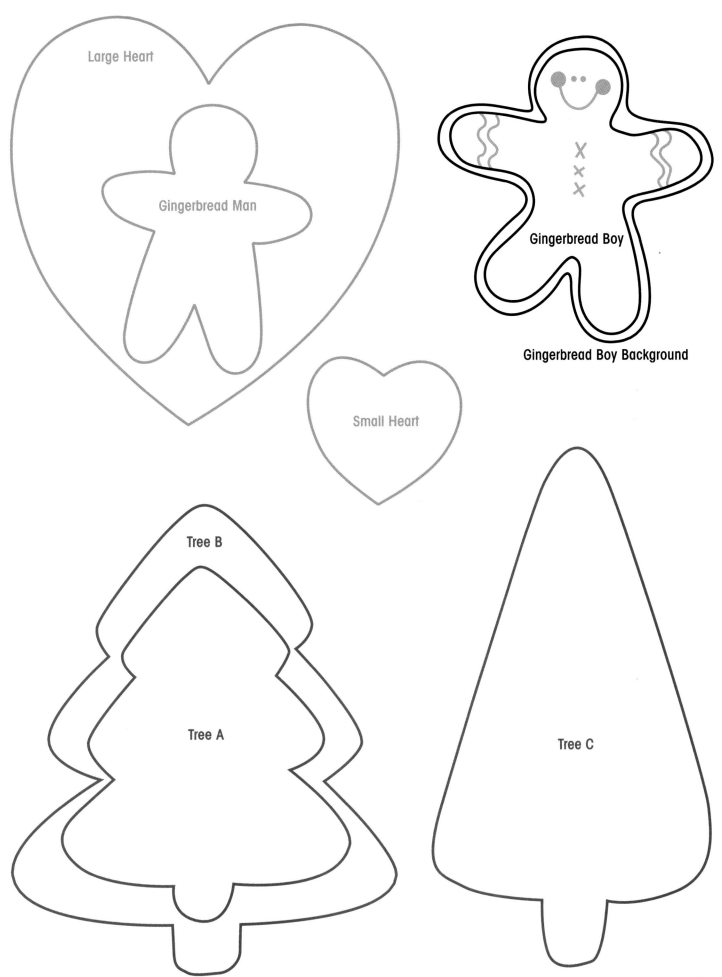

Large Heart

Gingerbread Man

Gingerbread Boy

Gingerbread Boy Background

Small Heart

Tree B

Tree A

Tree C

Hat

Scarf

Snowman

Tree

Tree Trunk

Coat

Face

Beard

Mitten A

Mitten B

Boots

Door

Heart

Leaf

Roof

Chimney

House Front

House Side

Scarf

Santa Hat Trim/Beard

cut out

Face

Snowman Hat Trim/Body

Snowman Hat

Broom

Santa Hat

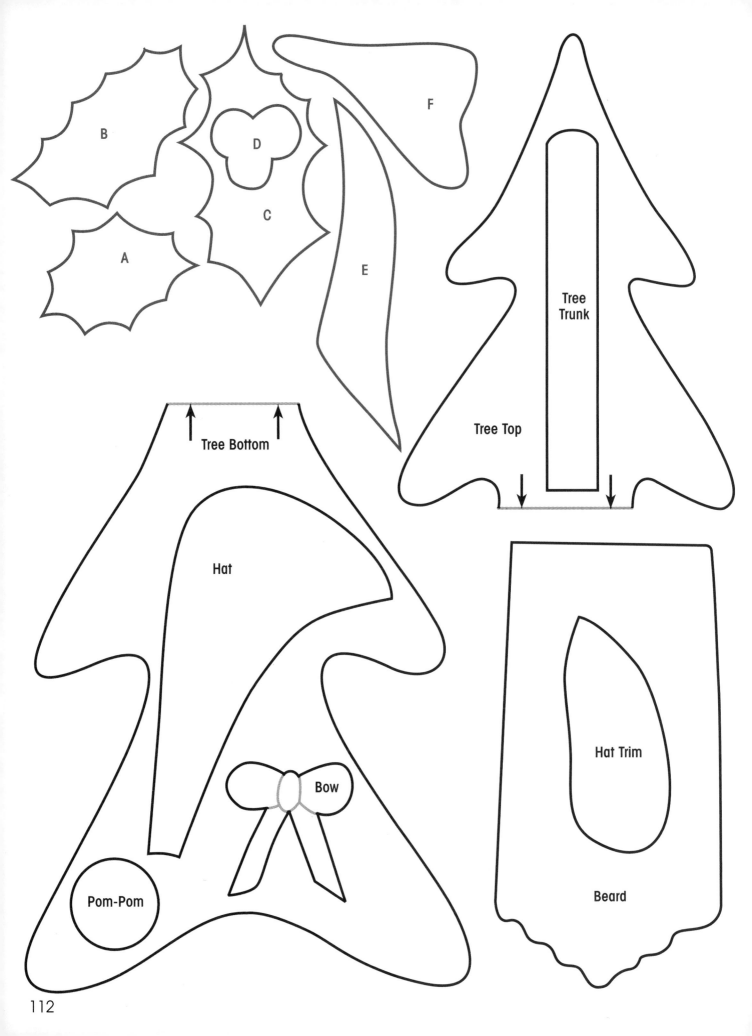

B

D

A

C

E

F

Tree Trunk

Tree Top

Tree Bottom

Hat

Hat Trim

Bow

Pom-Pom

Beard

Star B

Star C

Star A

Face

Pointed Star

Heart

Cuff

Mitten Tip

Mitten

113

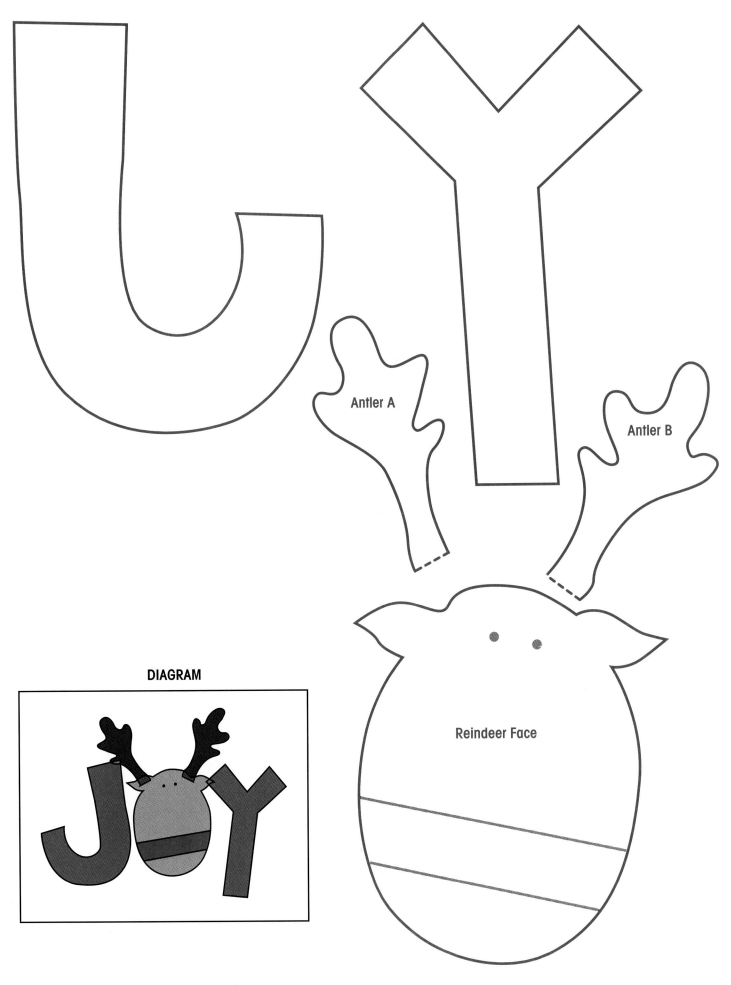

**DIAGRAM**

Antler A

Antler B

Reindeer Face

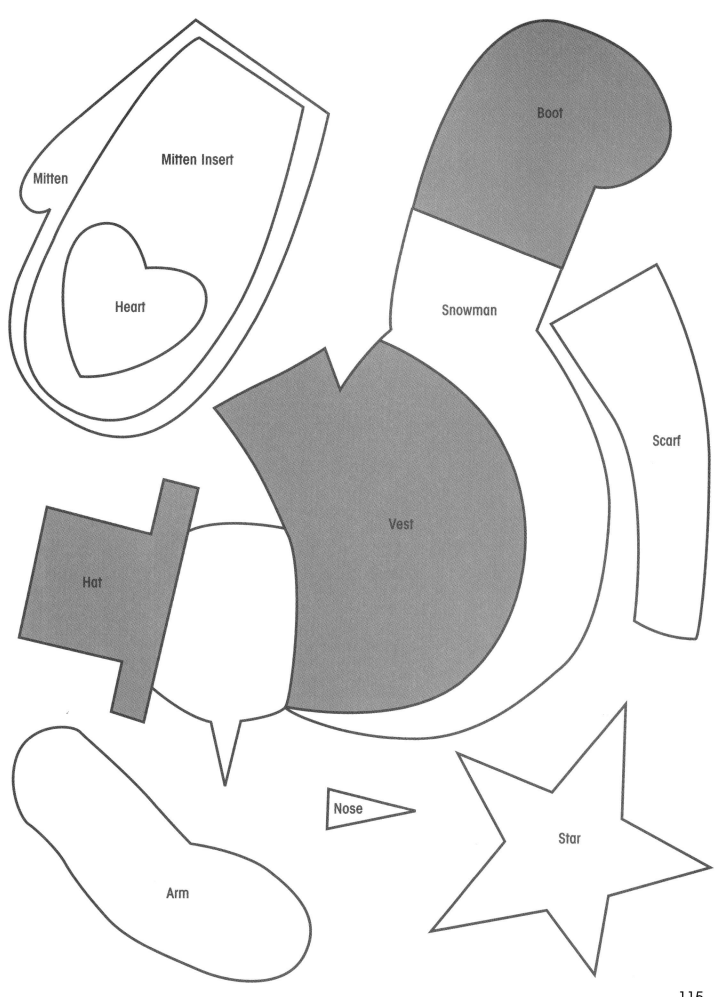

Mitten Insert

Mitten

Heart

Boot

Snowman

Scarf

Vest

Hat

Nose

Star

Arm

Angel Head

Wings

Star B

Star A

Ear A    Ear B

Reindeer Body Base

Reindeer
Head Base

Nose

Hoof A    Hoof B

Medium
Star

Small Star

Sleigh

Sleigh Base

Runner

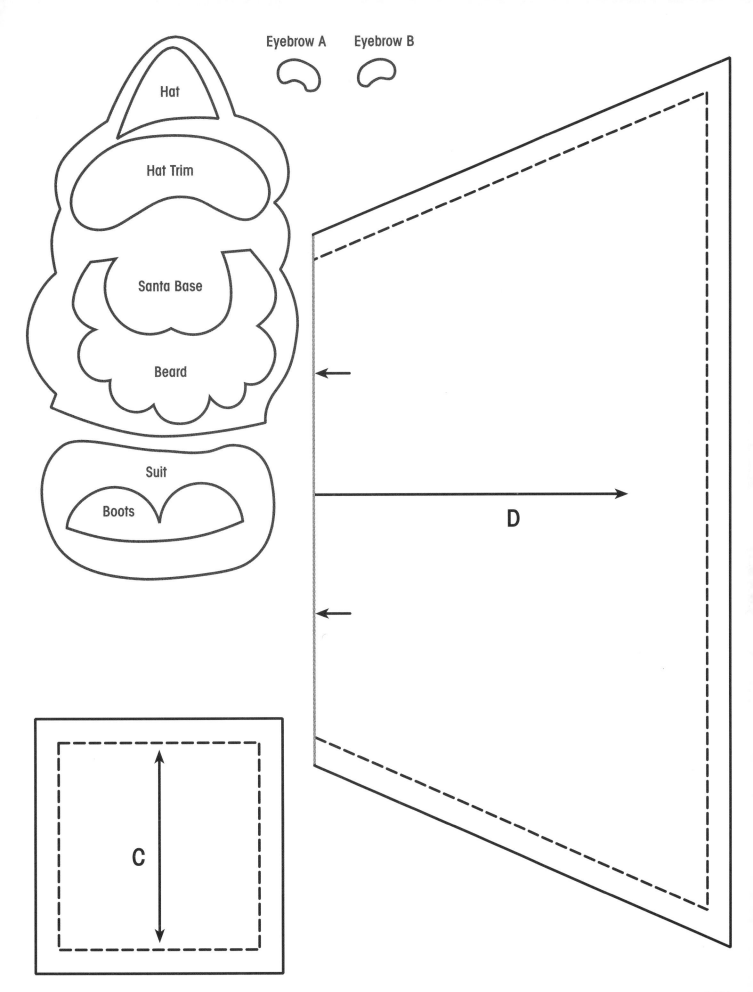

Hat

Eyebrow A    Eyebrow B

Hat Trim

Santa Base

Beard

Suit

Boots

D

C

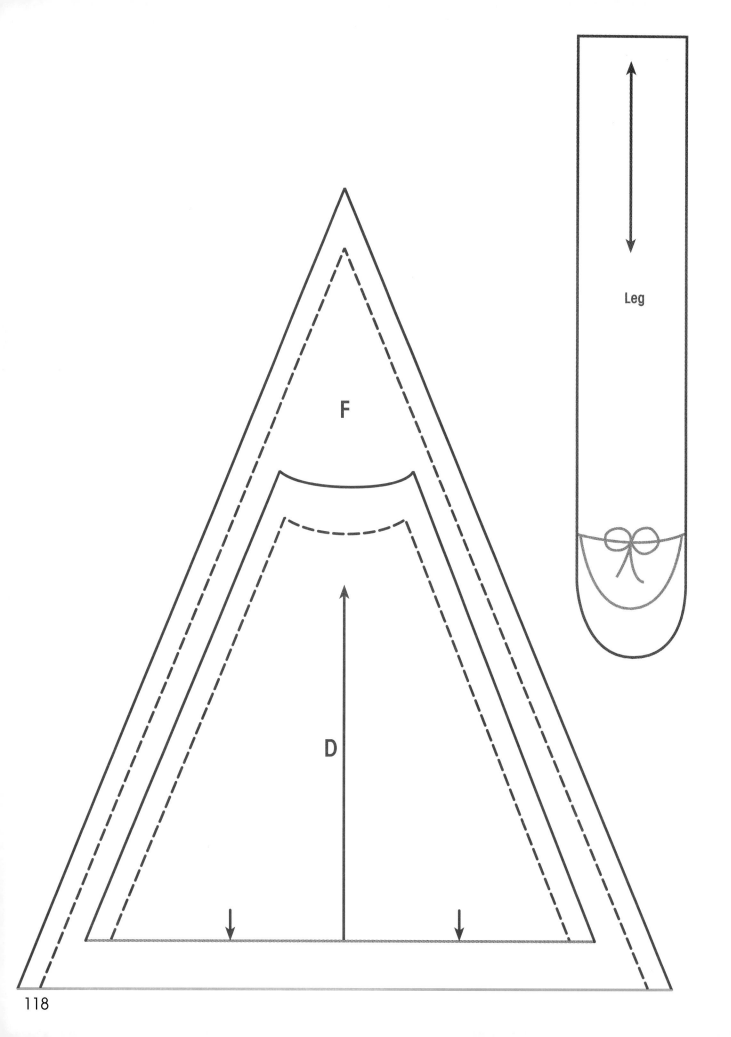

F

D

Leg

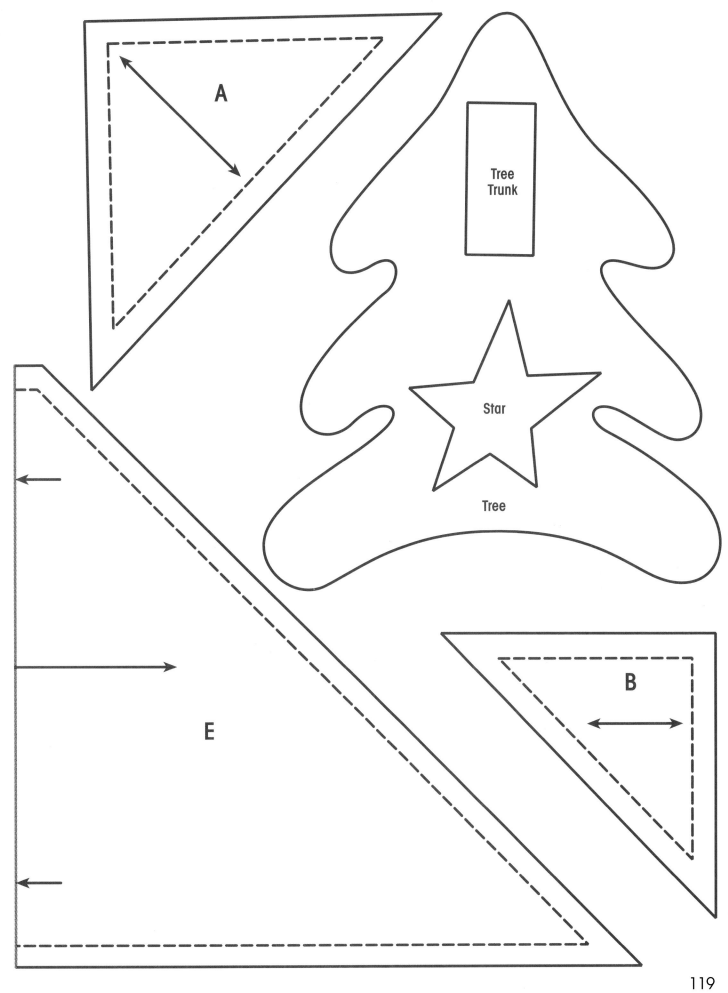

A

Tree
Trunk

Star

Tree

B

E

119

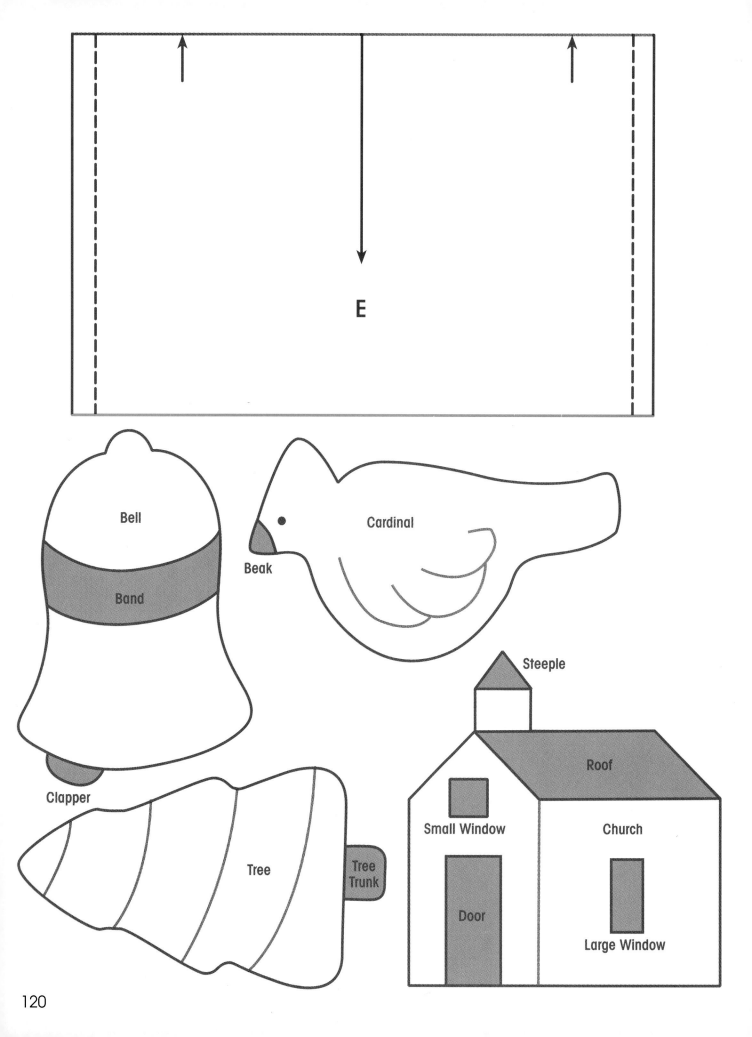

E

Bell

Band

Clapper

Beak

Cardinal

Steeple

Roof

Small Window

Church

Door

Large Window

Tree

Tree
Trunk

120

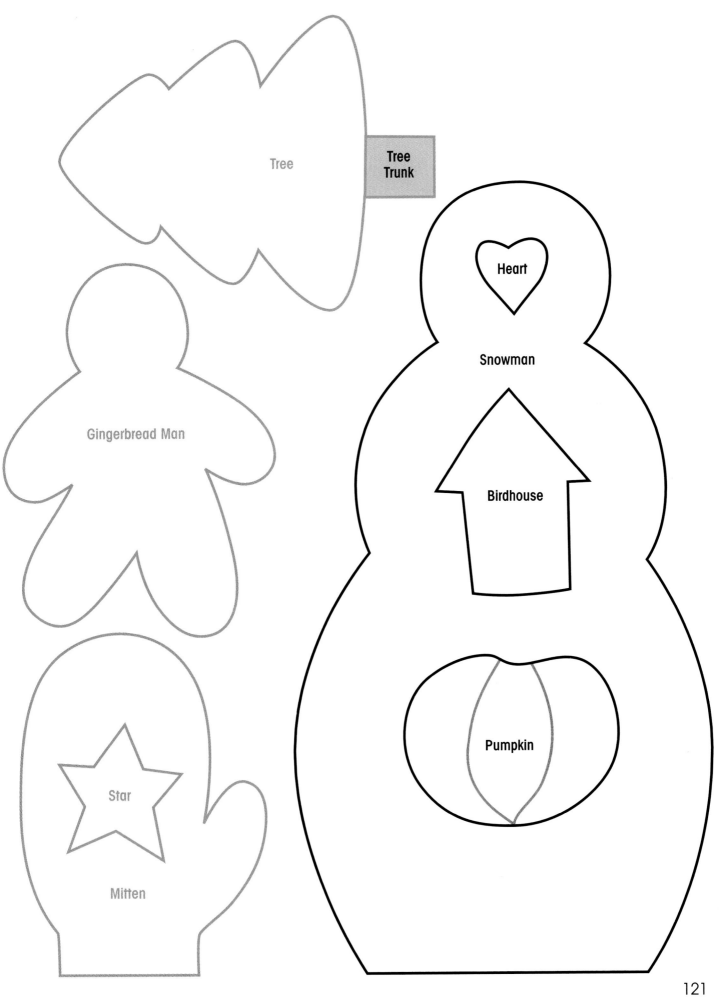

Tree

Tree
Trunk

Heart

Snowman

Birdhouse

Gingerbread Man

Star

Pumpkin

Mitten

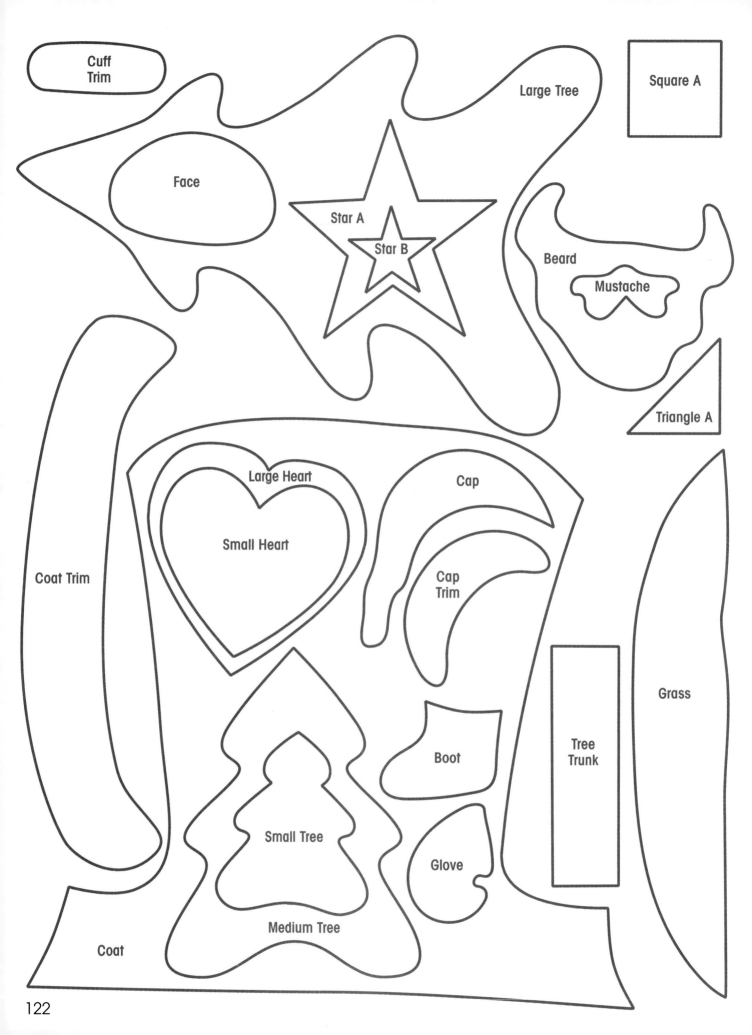

Cuff Trim

Large Tree

Square A

Face

Star A

Star B

Beard

Mustache

Triangle A

Large Heart

Cap

Small Heart

Coat Trim

Cap Trim

Grass

Boot

Tree Trunk

Small Tree

Glove

Medium Tree

Coat

122

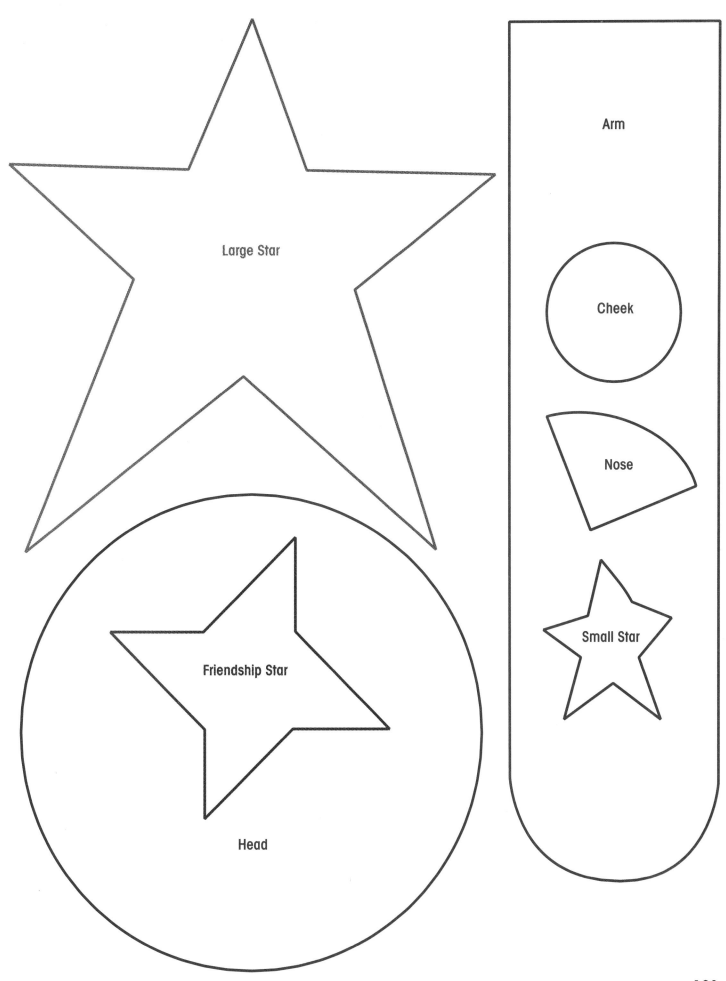

Large Star

Arm

Cheek

Nose

Small Star

Friendship Star

Head

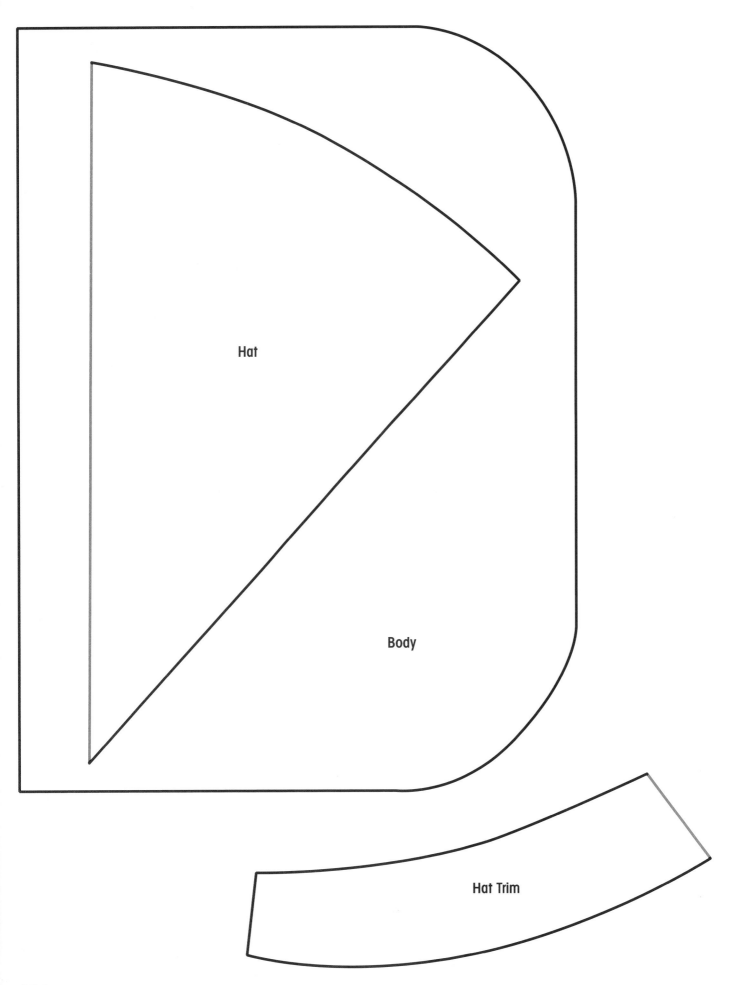

Hat

Body

Hat Trim

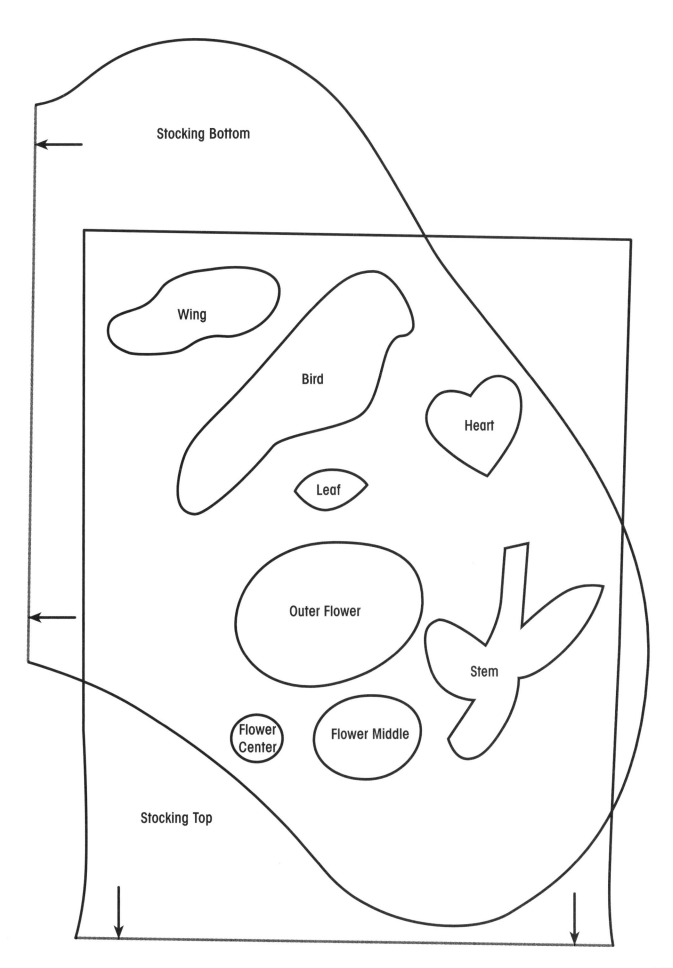

Stocking Bottom

Wing

Bird

Heart

Leaf

Outer Flower

Stem

Flower Center

Flower Middle

Stocking Top

125

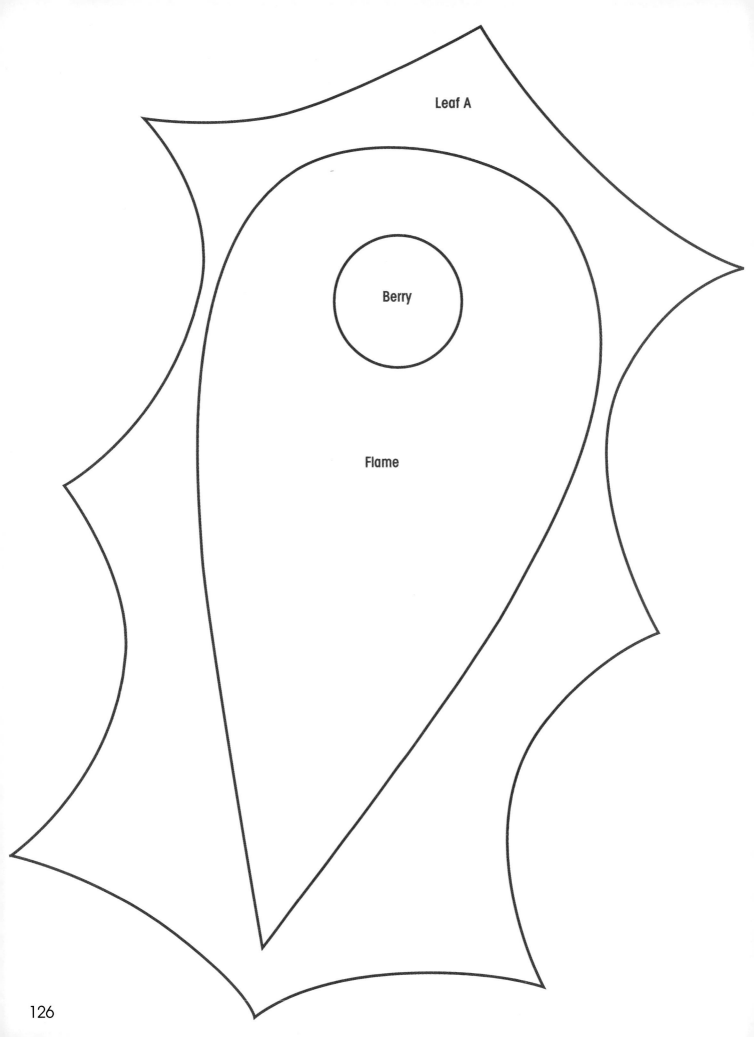

Leaf A

Berry

Flame

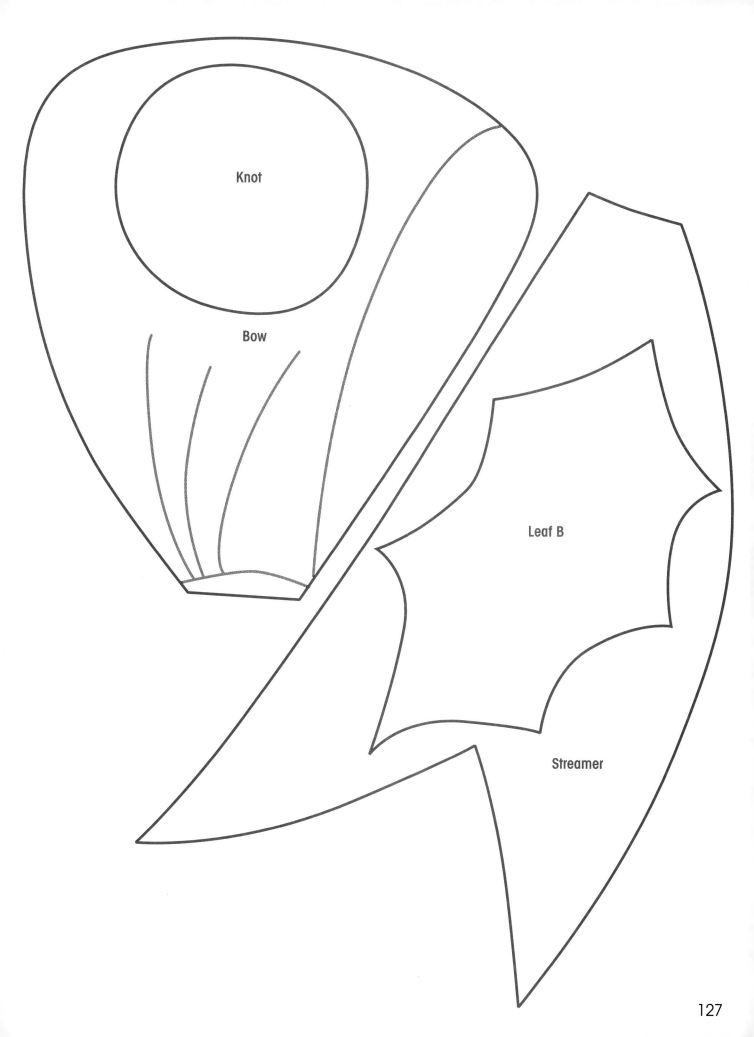

Knot

Bow

Leaf B

Streamer

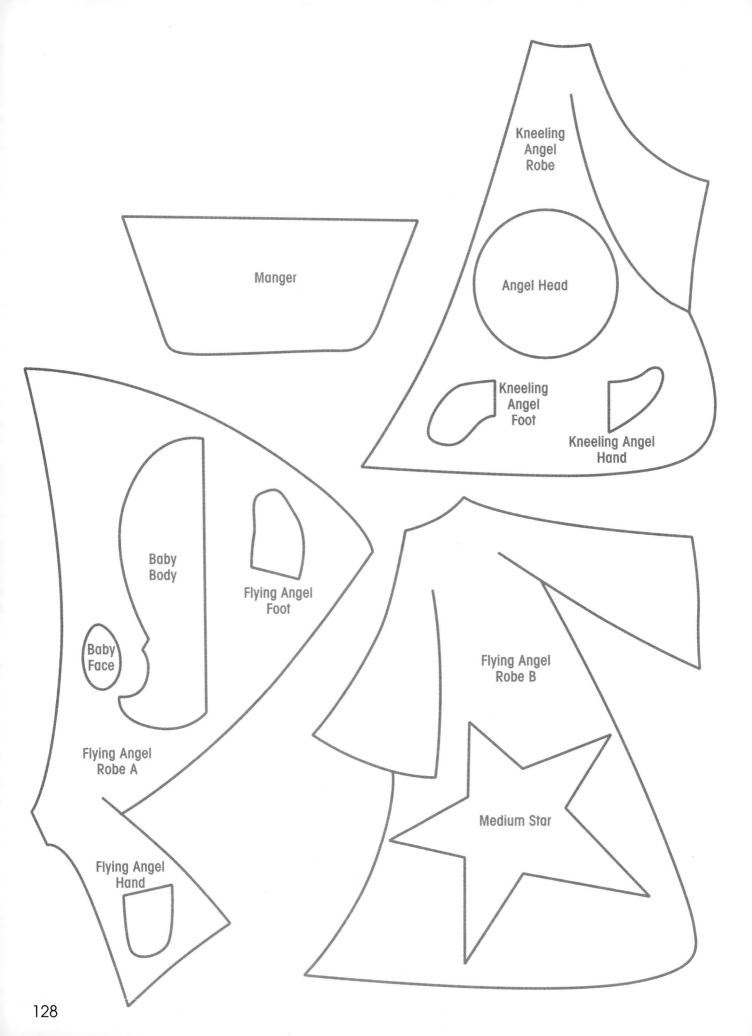

Kneeling
Angel
Robe

Angel Head

Kneeling
Angel
Foot

Kneeling Angel
Hand

Manger

Baby
Body

Flying Angel
Foot

Baby
Face

Flying Angel
Robe B

Flying Angel
Robe A

Medium Star

Flying Angel
Hand

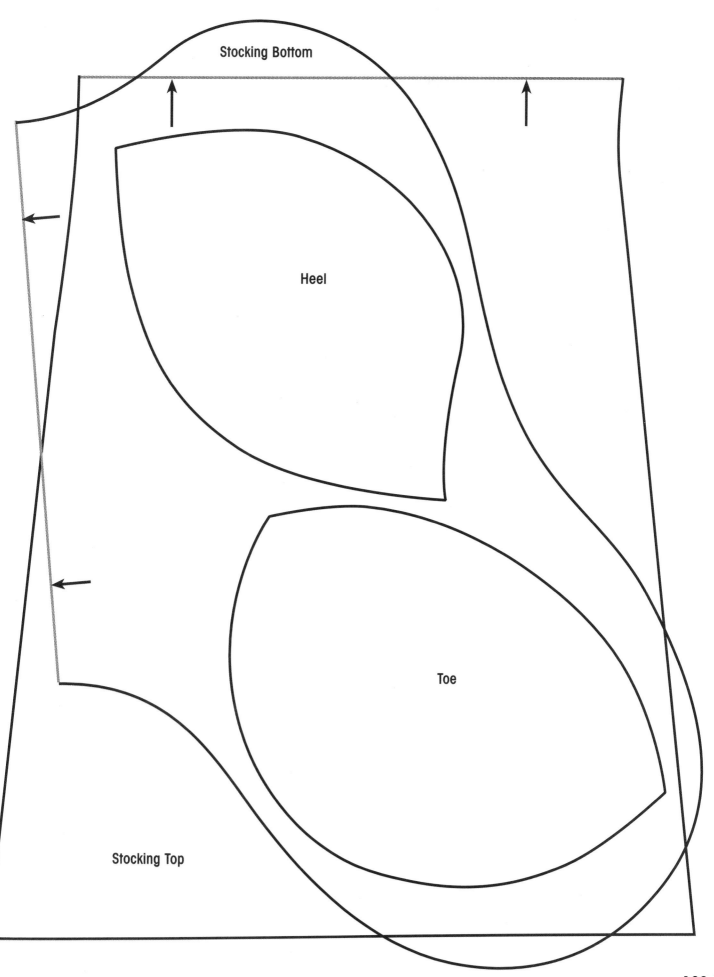

Stocking Bottom

Heel

Toe

Stocking Top

129

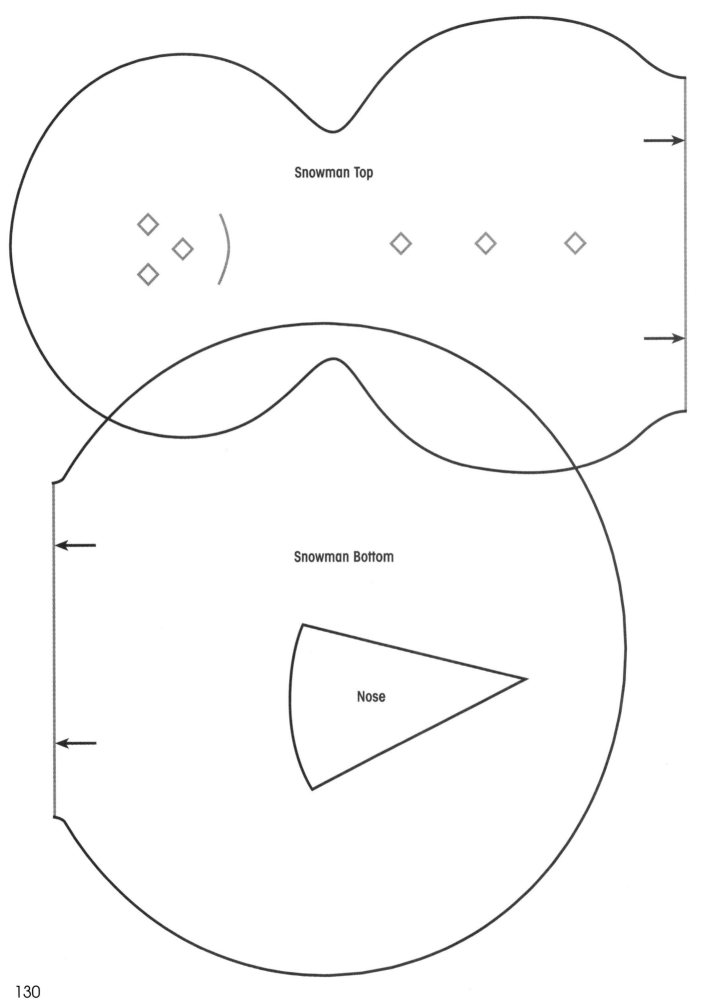

Snowman Top

Snowman Bottom

Nose

Leaf A

Leaf B

C

B

A

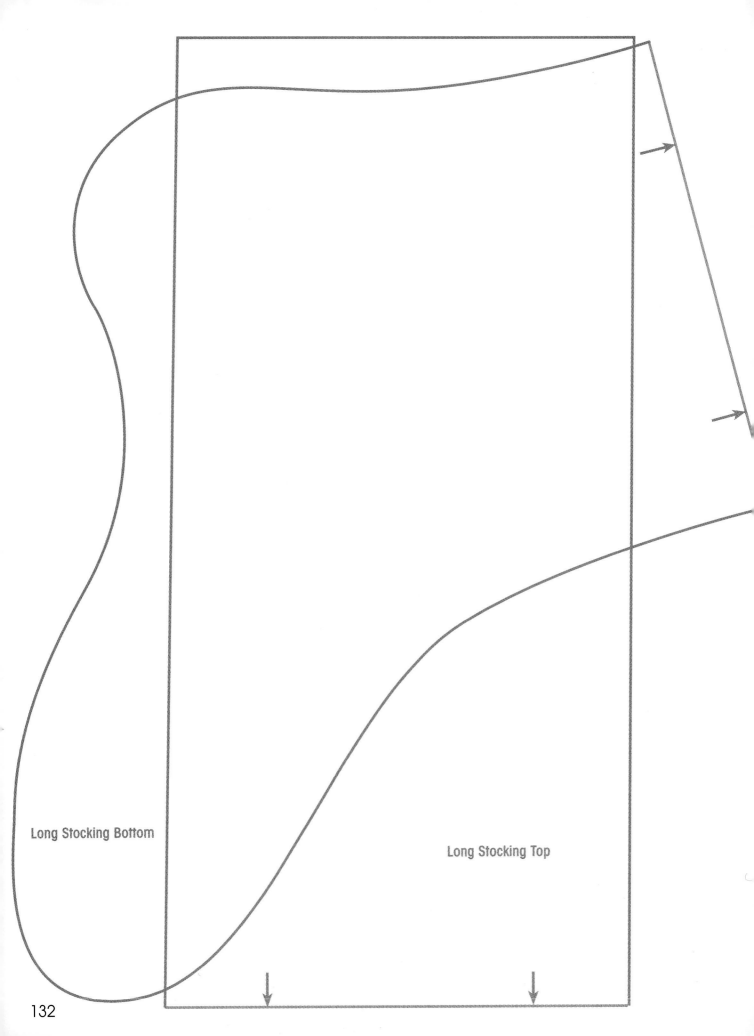

Long Stocking Bottom

Long Stocking Top

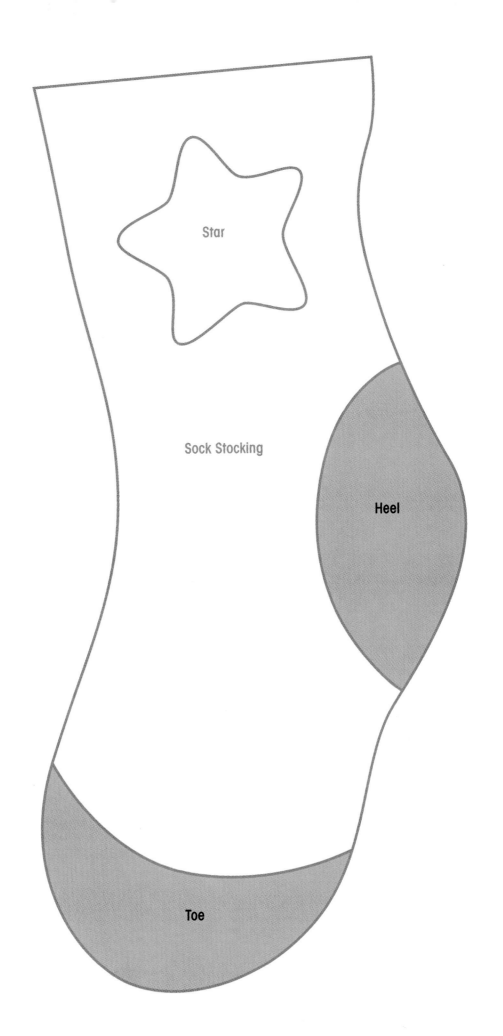

Star

Sock Stocking

Heel

Toe

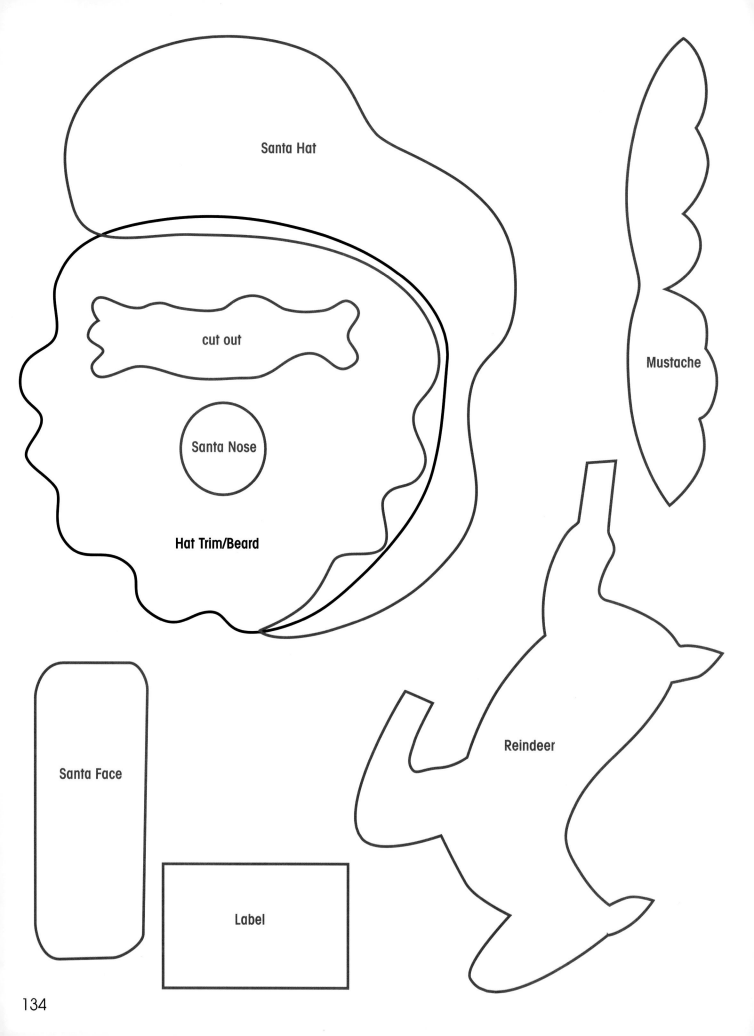

Santa Hat

cut out

Mustache

Santa Nose

Hat Trim/Beard

Reindeer

Santa Face

Label

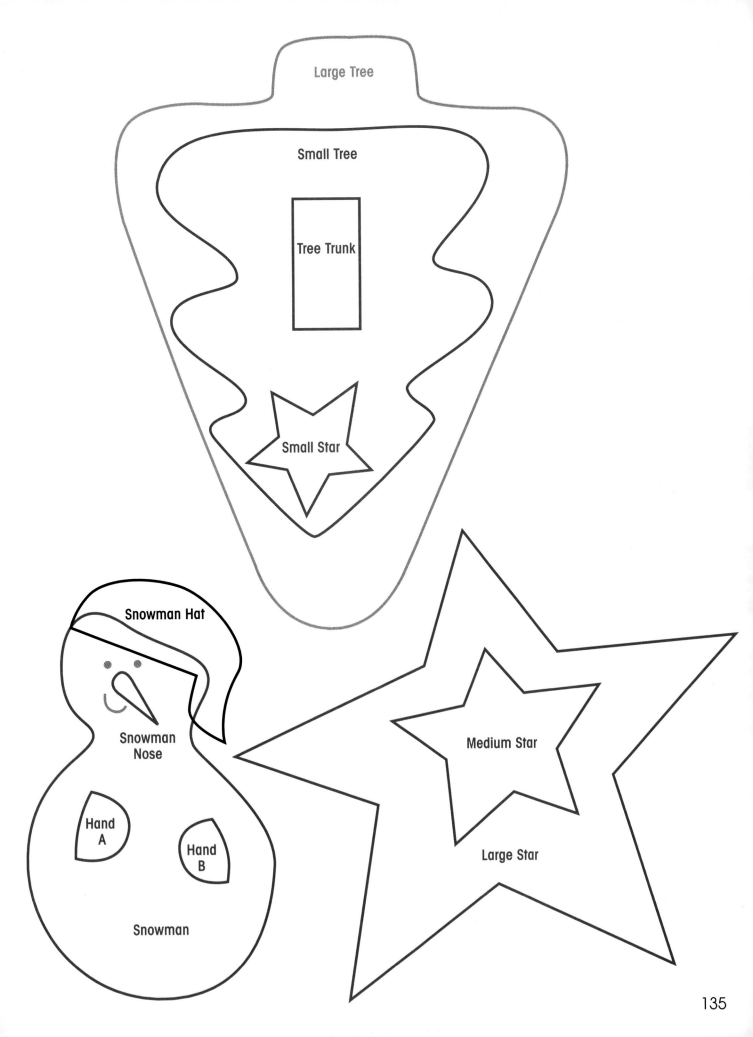

Large Tree

Small Tree

Tree Trunk

Small Star

Snowman Hat

Snowman Nose

Hand A

Hand B

Snowman

Medium Star

Large Star

135

Flower

Snowman Hat

Snowman Tie

Eye

Snow Lady Tie

Holly

Pipe

Snowman Head

Nose

Snow Lady Hat

136

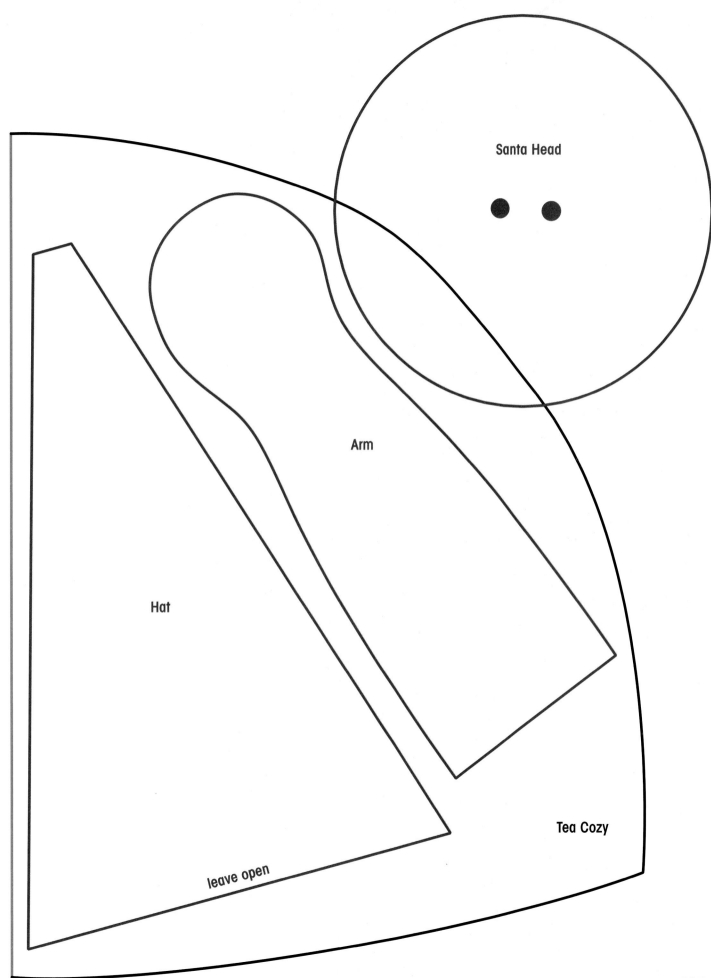

Santa Head

Arm

Hat

Tea Cozy

leave open

Tree Topper

Mitten

Small Star

Tree Trunk

Medium Star

Large Star

Yuletide Memories

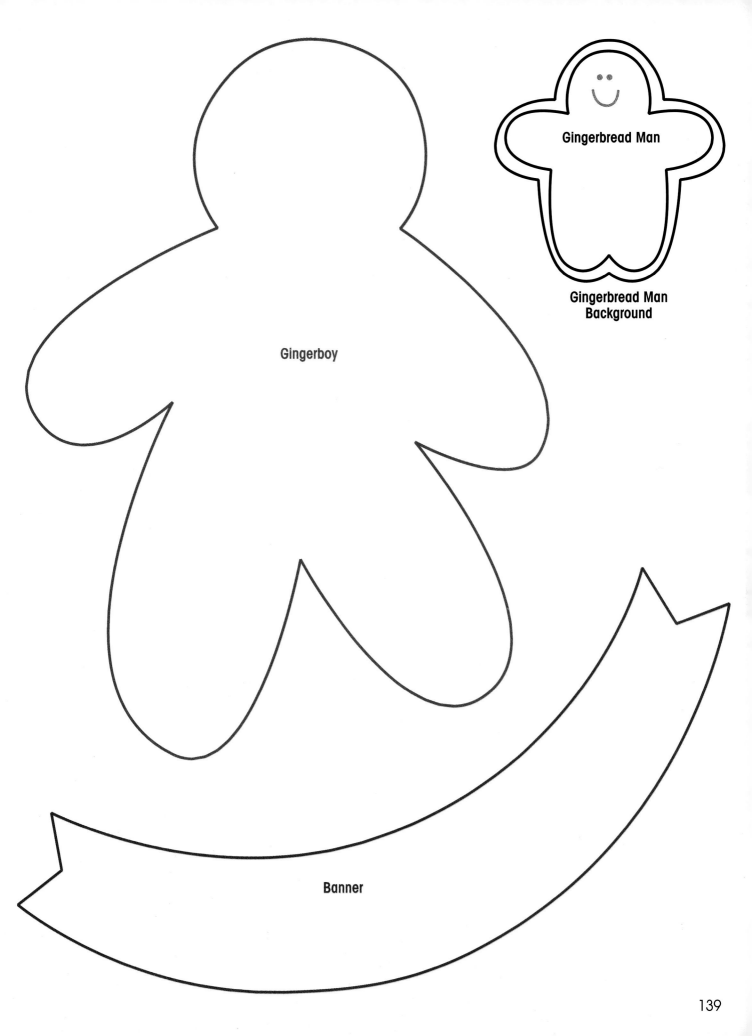

Gingerbread Man

Gingerbread Man
Background

Gingerboy

Banner

139

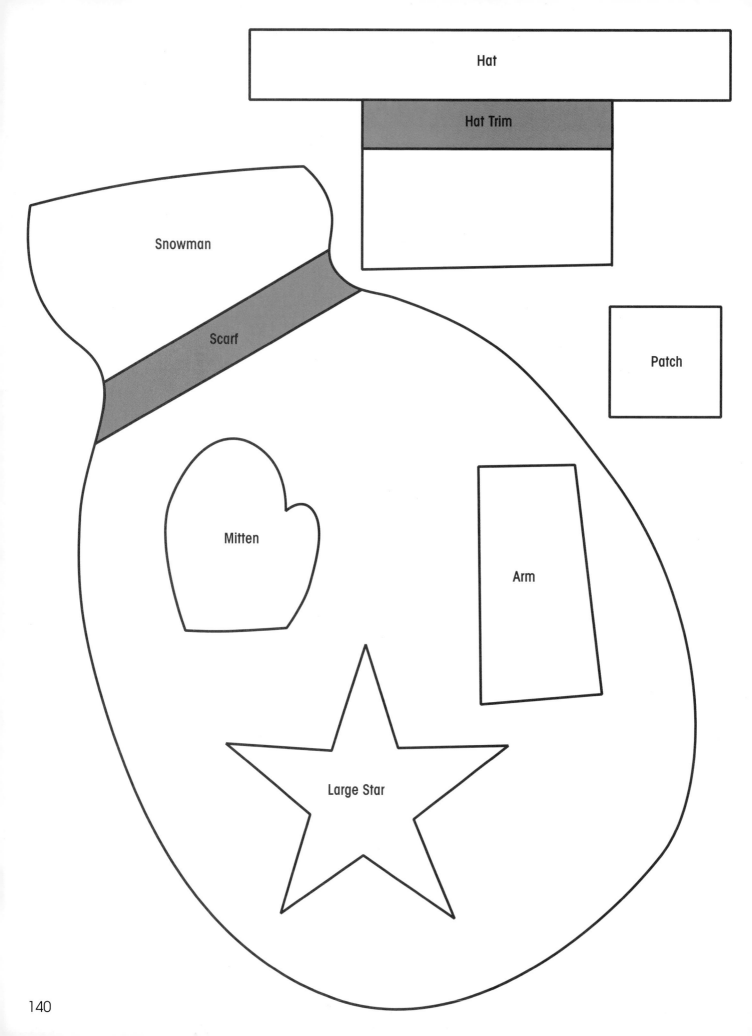

Hat

Hat Trim

Snowman

Scarf

Patch

Mitten

Arm

Large Star

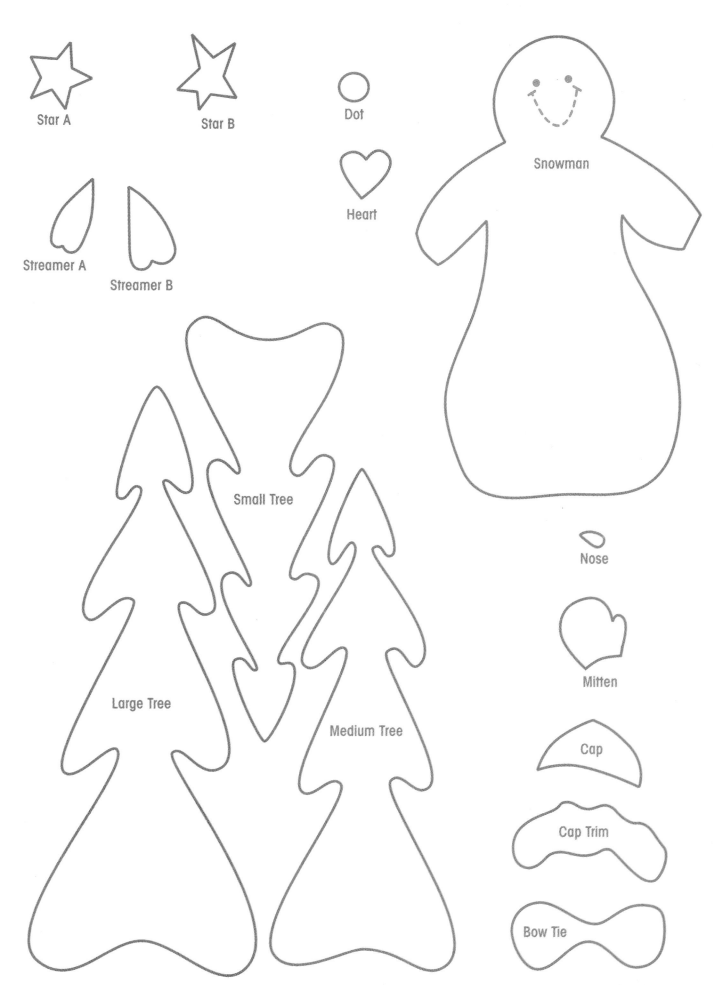

Star A

Star B

Dot

Snowman

Streamer A

Streamer B

Heart

Small Tree

Nose

Large Tree

Mitten

Medium Tree

Cap

Cap Trim

Bow Tie

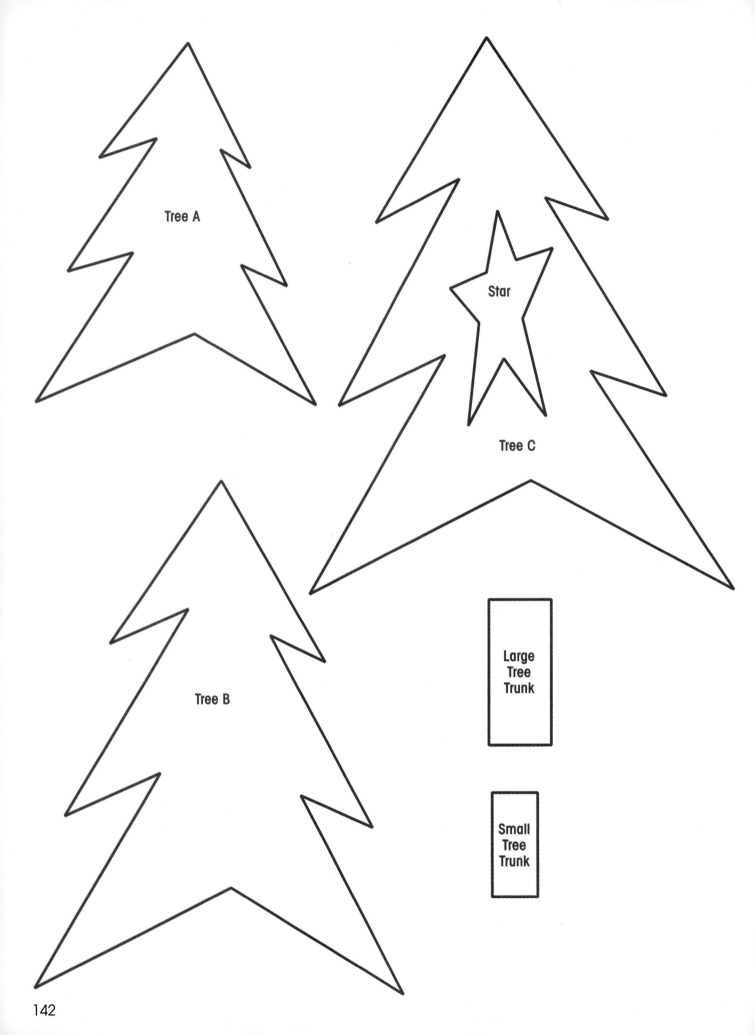

Tree A

Star

Tree C

Tree B

Large
Tree
Trunk

Small
Tree
Trunk